COLLECTING
Disneyana

IDENTIFICATION & VALUE GUIDE

The MICKEY MOUSE FIRE BRIGADE

By WALT DISNEY

DAVID LONGEST

COLLECTOR BOOKS

A Division of Schroeder Publishing Co., Inc.

On the front cover: Tinkerbell contemporary doll, 1930s Mickey Mouse Fisher Price pull toy, Mickey Mouse Fire Brigade storybook from the 1930s, Mickey and Minnie Mouse 1930s tin lithographed tray by Happy Nak of England, Walt Disney Classics Club Ariel and Pinocchio contemporary figures, and Mickey Mouse 1930s Ohio Art sand pail.

On the back cover: Mickey and Minnie Mouse 1930s Ohio Art sand pail, contemporary Alice in Wonderland doll with stand, 1980s Cheshire Cat ceramic figure, 1940s Steiff Bambi doll with original ear tag, and a large 1930s tin Mickey Mouse spinning top lithographed with early Disney characters.

Cover design by Beth Summers
Book design by Marty Turner
Cover photography by Charles R. Lynch

COLLECTOR BOOKS
P.O. Box 3009
Paducah, Kentucky 42002-3009

www.collectorbooks.com

Copyright © 2008 David Longest

The prices in this guide are derived by the author, wholly independent of the Walt Disney Company, and the Walt Disney Company has no connection therewith.

This book makes reference to "Mickey Mouse" and other various characters and films produced by the Walt Disney Company. All of the Disney characters and films are copyrighted by the Walt Disney Company. The characters also serve as trademarks of the Walt Disney Company.

The current values in this book should be used only as a guide. They are not intended to set prices, which vary from one section of the country to another. Auction prices as well as dealer prices vary greatly and are affected by condition as well as demand. Neither the author nor the publisher assumes responsibility for any losses that might be incurred as a result of consulting this guide.

SEARCHING FOR A PUBLISHER?

We are always looking for people knowledgeable within their fields. If you feel that there is a real need for a book on your collectible subject and have a large comprehensive collection, contact Collector Books.

Proudly printed and bound in the
United States of America

CONTENTS

ACKNOWLEDGMENTS

THIS BOOK MARKS A HAPPY RETURN FOR ME TO THE world of antique toy writing. I would personally like to thank both Bill Schroeder and Billy Schroeder for their faith in my projects over the years. Back in 1983 when I was a relative novice to the collecting world with only a couple of national antique toy articles to my credit, they put their faith in me. Now, 24 years later, I have written six books on antique toys for Collector Books and have two new titles being released this year. For their support and encouragement, I will always be grateful.

I would also like to thank both Gail Ashburn, editor, and Amy Sullivan, assistant editor, at Collector Books for the seemingly impossible and often thankless task of turning the stacks of hundreds of photos and layout pages into something that is now a book. Your work and designs are always amazing, and this author thanks you from the bottom of his heart for making him look good…and sometimes even intelligent.

To my wife, Ann, thanks for the prodding that kept me at my computer as deadlines approached and for the endless understanding that living with a toy collector means enduring the habits of a kid who never grew up. I am thankful that you have shared my hobby for the past 27 years of our marriage and put up with it even when we were dating as college kids. It was tempting to just sit on the floor and play with our golden retrievers all evening, but you always encouraged me to get back to the task at hand. No writer ever had a better coach, or wife. Mark Twain's wife Livvy did the very same thing. He may have done all the writing, but it was a steadfast wife who kept him on task and made sure he produced something. So, for all the great wives out there and personal coaches, I thank you. And I thank my own. Love you.

For Claire, my daughter, who is now a musical theatre student at Otterbein College in Columbus, Ohio, and the true inspiration of my seemingly crazed lunacy to write two books at once, may you watch your old dad grow old gracefully surrounded by childhood playthings. Like Peter Pan, I just never grew up, and when your teenaged friends came to call and realized that your father was somehow a little "different," you were always gracious and understanding. I thank you for that. To my Mom, I'm glad you are still around to see yet another work of mine through to the end. I'm not sure why you kept all of my books over all these years except for the same reason any parents save old baseball gloves, ice skates, trophies, artwork, and yes, old toys. Thanks for being there for me all these years.

Finally, to Elmer and Viola Reynolds of Martinsville, Indiana, thank you for your forever friendship. If I hadn't been shut out at that auction in rural Indiana some 26 years ago and you hadn't bid upon and won that huge old showcase that was far too large for any one person to carry down your basement stairs, we would never have met. And think of all the museum openings, antique shows, St. Charles Antique Toy World shows, Indianapolis Antique Advertising Shows, country auctions, flea markets, and evenings of "Show and Tell" that we would have missed together. Your collecting passions fueled my own, and after a quarter of a century, it's still fun to know that you are far more than friends could ever be, you are dear family. My books would not exist without your input, your knowledge, your enthusiasm, and yes, your fantastic toys. Thank you, thank you, thank you!

I would also like to thank the following persons, publications, and institutions who have helped educate me as a writer and a collector for over 30 years: Ted Hake, Tom Tumbusch, Michael Stern, George Hattersley, The Children's Museum of Indianapolis, William and Mary Furnish, Dave and Elaine Hughes, Terry Stewart and Stewart Promotions, Doug Moore and the Indianapolis Antique Advertising Show, Bob Coup, Herb Smith and Smith House Auctions, Dale Kelly and both *Antique Toy World Magazine* and Antique World Toy Shows, Keith and Donna Kaonis with *Collector's Showcase Magazine*, Kyle Husfloen and *Toy Shop Magazine*, *The Antique Trader* magazine, *The Tri-State Trader*, Indiana University and Indiana University Southeast, Dr. Richard Brengle, Bob Bernabe, Joe Reese, Helene and Stewart Pollack, Jim Miller, Butch and Linda Miller, Jane Eberle, Harry and Jean Hall, Tommy Hall, Mel Birnkrandt, Maurice Sendak, Mike and Gina Sullivan, Bernie Shine, Steve Quertermous,

Les Fish, Keith Spurgeon, Maxine and Stuart Evans, Andrea Evans, Brimfield Antique Shows of Brimfield, Massachusetts, and anybody else who I might have forgotten.

And to collectors new to the world of Disneyana collecting and those who have been at it for decades like myself, may we all never forget that, in the words of Walt Disney himself, "It all started with a mouse." Every time we all meet in front of the castle at Walt Disney World, Disneyland, or any of the other Disney theme parks, let's not forget that our passion for the hunt of that which is Disney is as American as apple pie or the girl next door. It's a unique forever young quest we have set out upon, and may that quest never end. Thanks to all who have helped make Disneyana collecting what it is today. And, in those immortal closing words delivered by The Mouse himself at the closing of each episode of *The Mickey Mouse Club* as we all hit the trail heading out into the collecting world, I hope to "See you real soon!"

— David Longest, February 2007

INTRODUCTION

WELCOME TO THE WORLD OF COLLECTING DISNEYANA. Some will come to these pages with a novice fascination for the color and the art of the toys themselves. Others will seek out the toys for a spark they rekindle in the memories of their own childhood. Still others may find a particular Disney character that has always struck their fancy and they are happy to stick with them. Whatever the reason, collecting Disneyana can be both a fun and highly rewarding hobby, not to mention even a strong investment.

Consider the possibilities: When I first began collecting Disneyana as a college student in the 1970s (1974 to be exact) there were only two Disney theme parks: Disneyland in California and Walt Disney World's Magic Kingdom in Florida. That was it. No European parks, no Epcot, no Animal Kingdom, no Disney's MGM Studios, certainly no California Adventure. There was no Internet, no eBay, very few specialty toy auction houses, hardly any toy publications devoted to antique toys and collecting, only a handful of antique toy shows, and a vast array of antique flea markets. There wasn't much of a choice. You either pounded the pavement at flea markets, read lengthy auction listings, or hoped to find toys at yard sales, estate sales, or country auctions. The very best you could hope for was the good fortune of making a lucky swap with a fellow local collector. That was it!

Thirty-three years later, collecting Disneyana is a whole new ball game. Or, in the words of Disney's Aladdin and Jasmine, it's "A Whole New World!" With the advent of the world-wide Internet and auction houses such as eBay, toy collecting has taken on a 24/7 reality...in truth, Disneyana collectors can buy and sell toys at any hour of any day, 365 days a year. Those simple times of running around like a pack rat at local flea markets have come and gone as both buyers and sellers have become more knowledgeable and price conscious. And when it comes to instant gratification, the Internet offers with it the option of purchasing a piece of early Disneyana at any hour of any day.

After 33 years and at least two dozen pairs of worn-out sneakers, I can speak of the benefits of both the old ways of acquiring great toys and certainly the new. Disneyana collectors are a unique specialized facet of all toy collectors because they each have in common a love for both Walt Disney himself and certainly Mickey Mouse. Both are American entities that seem pretty pointless when only surveyed for their cultural impact or monetary worth in the collecting marketplace. Collecting Disneyana and Walt Disney collectibles just for sheer investment goals or the value of the toys themselves misses the point. It's an empty pursuit. You could do better with stocks and bonds, or gold in the long run as a capital

investment. There must be an emotional connection. Either you love the "Disney dream" and the toys help you connect with it, or you don't. It's as simple as that. My guess is that you have that connection or you wouldn't have turned through the pages of this book to begin with. Walt Disney himself remains much more than an entertainment icon today; he is an American institution as remarkable as Babe Ruth, Abe Lincoln, or Wall Street. His persona is associated with every piece of Disneyana collected, not because he actually appears as a likeness in the toys, but because his influence upon the characters he created was as much an alter-ego of his own imagination as if he had named Mickey and the rest of the gang after himself or his own family members.

When Disneyana collectors gather, conversation usually centers upon recent trips to "the parks" where nearly all collectors eventually migrate like homing pigeons with mouseketeer hats, or upon Walt himself. Disney, the man, is like a folk hero grandfather to us all. Or maybe a fun great uncle. Or both. As children, we sat in front of our brand new color televisions (if our families were lucky enough to own one!) and anxiously awaited the Sunday evening presentations of *Walt Disney's Wonderful World of Color*. We would gather, a nation of youngsters and their parents, awaiting the immortal wisdom of "Walt" as he would stand at his office desk, sometimes with an animated friend at his side who would actually converse with him or sometimes he would just play to a model of a familiar character friend he was about to introduce for the evening. Whatever the case, we were spellbound, transfixed, visually glued to the television. We were hooked. Our own imaginations hung upon his every word. There we sat, for a full hour each Sunday night, riveted to whatever subject matter Uncle Walt had chosen for us that evening. It might be a *True Life Adventure*, a sort of Disneyized version of a National Geographic film usually featuring cute animals which included an animal behavior lesson with an upbeat Disney spin on things, or it might be an actual two-part evening of a Disney feature film which would air half on one Sunday night and the second half the following week. It didn't matter. There were no dvds, no videos, no cable channels. Whatever Walt Disney had selected for us that evening was fine. It was the only Disney fix we would get for that week, and it was enough. We would have to muddle through five more days of school, seven more days of waiting, a whole busy week of 1960s life until our next Sunday night visit with our favorite surrogate grandfather. And life went on.

Whatever would be shown each week on *Disney's Wonderful World of Color* didn't matter. Whatever

would be shown, it bore Walt's stamp of approval and it would be totally Disney and pure fun. Every week. Same time, same quality family entertainment, same night, same Walt, without question. And why wouldn't we watch? Walt was as important to our lives as Babe Ruth had been a generation earlier. Walt had delivered.

When it was "hip" to bash conservatism, family values, and the gentler postwar generation days of the "Ozzie and Harriet" (another 1950s fine family entertainment show) mentality, Walt's steadfast family entertainment stand took some knocks. Some criticized the Disney studio as too family oriented, too milky white wholesome, too sweet, too formula. But those same counter culture critics who might lash out at the studio for churning out predictable family hits like *Swiss Family Robinson* or *Old Yeller* still wore Mickey Mouse watches on their wrists as they typed their pages of criticism. They might not have liked the formula at Disney in the 1960s because by that time, maybe little kids just weren't cool. But Mickey Mouse never faded. Love him or leave him, Mickey's image led the pop culture counter revolution with his image plastered all over the place with images of "pop art" now being way too cool. So, in a twist of fate and pure irony, his renaissance led to the current fascination with vintage Disneyana collecting which started in the late 1960s and has not faltered even today, some 40 years later!

For nearly 30 years from the 1930s through the 1960s, Walt had delivered. He revolutionized family entertainment at the movies and on television. This was the man who had brought us Mary Poppins, Disneyland, and Sunday night cartoons on prime time television…in color! *Bonanza* would appear an hour or two later each Sunday night, but the *Wonderful World of Color* kept toddlers up until bedtime, and they watched with mom and dad looking on, all together as a family. There was no escape. We were all hooked. And now, some four decades later, we still surround ourselves with toys in the likenesses of these familiar old friends. It's like gathering old family back into our fold. And so, we collect.

The purpose of this book is to reunite the Disney fan family with a selection of great old toys from 80 years of Disney character merchandising. This book is by no means the last word in collecting Disneyana. Great volumes by other authors have preceded it, and greater ones will likely follow. But for this stop-frame of time, this new volume is intended to give both advanced and novice collectors alike some advice on maintaining and preserving your collections, what to pay for toys in the current marketplace, suggestions on displaying them, and where the future of Disneyana collecting is headed

in general. I am by no means the ultimate authority as a singular author on collecting all things Disney. As I have previously mentioned, I have been joyfully at it for some 33 years now, and I suppose that makes me one of the old timers in the collecting field. I have seen the fads relating to Disneyana collecting come and go. I have pursued my own sirens of collecting pogs, pins, reproduction art, limited edition sericels, Disney Beanie Babies, autograph books, and you name it — and like Ulysses, I have always returned home…to the toys. The antique and vintage Disneyana toys have always remained the standard of all that is good about collecting objects related to the industry created by Walt. It always comes back to Walt.

No matter how old I get, Walt Disney still remains on my top five list at the fantasy dinner table. We all muse about this from time to time. My list of fantasy dinner guests is, in no particular order: Jesus, Thomas Jefferson, John Kennedy, Babe Ruth, and, of course, Walt Disney. All of these gentlemen together at one table would certainly make for some interesting and unusual conversation. Certainly religion, spirituality, and reason would fill the first hour of talk. But then, as everyone enjoyed dessert, somebody would ask Ruth how he managed to do what he did, and his answer would be short as he stuffed more desserts into his mouth. Then somebody would ask Walt the inevitable question, how he feels about the current direction of his namesake company, Disney.

I think Walt would see the humor and ultimate irony in his corporation now owning ABC, the very same network that Walt had to nearly sell himself to in order to get Disneyland on the air in the 1950s. That black and white early television series was pretty primitive by the later *World of Color* series standards and even more archaic when compared to today's high definition Disney Channel standards, but it was great stuff for its day. And the weekly airing of whatever Disney chose to "promote" on the *Disneyland* program allowed Americans to experience early on and first hand what promising new inventions, theme park features, movie releases, or scientific advancements were on the horizon that Walt himself had discovered or had planned for us. It was Walt and ABC partnering over half a century ago that had established the Disney Studios into the forefront of family entertainment. As he would munch on a piece of apple pie at the fantasy dinner table, I think Walt would pause and relish the knowledge that Disney now owns that network!

As collectors young and old make their way through these pages, it is my hope that the photographs and the information presented here will inspire yet another generation to continue to collect all that is great in art

and design about Disney characters. The price guide presented throughout the photo captions is at best a general one. I have used the e/mv value code which breaks down to the first price listed being the current average value estimate for that particular toy pictured as found in excellent condition, and the second value listed is the value of the toy in today's collector marketplace as found in mint condition. If a toy is pictured with its original box, then assume the values relate to that toy in as-pictured condition, with its original box. If no original packaging or boxing is photographed, then assume the values are for the toy pictured without its box. This pricing takes into account recent trends in Disneyana collecting. Certainly the Internet has made even extremely rare examples of Disneyana easier to find with instant access, but with this immediacy comes what I regard as "price volatility." Internet auction sites are useful, but sometimes very fickle when it comes to using prices realized at auction to establish true worth or value of a particular toy. A rare Disneyana windup toy that sells for $2,000 on a given Tuesday night when no bidder out there seems to be at home or available to bid might sell for $3,500 at prime time on a Saturday night closing sale when several competing bidders have discovered it. The fact that the same toy in the same condition might have sold with a comparative $1,500 value spread doesn't tell us that the toy's value has changed, it simply illustrates that in the collecting world, particularly among rare and antique toys (and this includes Disneyana), toy values are market driven. As always, it is immediate supply and demand. It's all a matter of how many people want a particular toy, and much and how badly they want to pay for it.

So use this value guide with its intended purpose in mind. It is a guide. Don't use it to appraise your entire collection because too many variables compete for an exact appraisal of any given item. Use the prices and the ranges presented here for your own reference to gauge an approximate value of what a given toy might cost you today in the marketplace at either a specialized antique toy show or a competitive Internet auction. It is this author's hope that you find you have acquired many of your toys at well below the market values presented here (known to us in the collecting world as "sleepers"), and may you find that many of your toys are worth exactly what you paid for them because you already knew that they had great value, rarity, and worth (known in the collecting world as "keepers").

May you find a king's ransom of both sleepers and keepers. In the world of Disneyana collecting, that's all you can hope for "When You Wish Upon A Star." Happy collecting in the days ahead!

THE GOLDEN YEARS
OF EARLY DISNEYANA

VISIT ANY DISNEY THEME PARK ON ANY GIVEN DAY and you will undoubtedly be met by swarms of Disney characters just inside the entrance gate. From the earliest inception of the parks, Walt Disney knew that visiting a theme park meant putting the public in touch with his beloved characters. For the past 50 years, a walk into a Disney theme park with a young child produces the instant necessity to purchase an autograph book. And you can buy them, immediately. Just as you step through the turnstiles, there are vendors standing at wagons ready to sell you a pen and an autograph pad. And that's just the way it should be. Disney marketing is all about that. See a need, then fill it. As soon as you step into Town Square at either Disneyland or Walt Disney World's Magic Kingdom, it is instantly obvious who the most popular Disney characters are. It has and will always remain the "Fab Five" as Disney enthusiasts know them: Mickey Mouse, Minnie Mouse, Donald Duck, Goofy, and Pluto. Mickey Mouse turns 80 next year along with Minnie, and the other three are just a year or two younger, but their fame lasts. And that is owed all to the ingenuity of Walt Disney himself for creating family entertainment characters who are timeless.

These "Fab Five" are responsible for making Disney marketing the successful business enterprise that it has been for seven decades. Walt Disney realized early on that there would be great public demand for his created characters, but it was not until his association began with businessman and marketing genius Kay Kamen that he realized the true scope of character merchandising. Kamen knew that the key to successful character merchandising meant tight, restrictive character licensing. And so he was able to seek out the leading toy, novelty, children's apparel, hobby, game, and even food manufacturers who were interested in boosting their own bottom lines by adding Disney character likenesses to their merchandising. Kamen was even able to create bidding wars between some first rate manufacturers to create an even greater interest in the Disney line

of characters to boost sales, and the Walt Disney Studios were the beneficiary of the residuals. Big character merchandising meant big copyright licensing fees for Walt Disney and his young company, and in the 1930s, no U.S. company marketed to the children's audience and consumer pool better than Kamen and Disney.

Today's collectors of vintage 1930s Disney character memorabilia know the benefits of the Kamen-Disney association. As a result of Kamen's marketing expertise, such substantial toy manufacturers of the 1930s as Ohio Art, Lionel, Louis Marx, Crown Toy and Novelty, Ideal, Knickerbocker, Milton Bradley, Marks Brothers of Boston, Whitman Publishing, Parker Brothers Games, American Toy Works, Fisher Price, and Hall Brothers Cards (later Hallmark) were brought into the Disney character merchandising family, to name only a few. And as collectors who love 1930s Disney character toys we must tip our hats to Disney for creating the characters. But, in truth, for creating the marketing that created the great toys, we owe it all to Kay Kamen.

Vintage Mickey collectors who specialize in 1930s Mickey and Minnie Mouse do so because in that singular decade, their look was unlike that of any other in history. After 1939, the Walt Disney Studios attempted to continually "modernize" the look of all their characters, even the "Fab Five." After about 1939, Mickey and Minnie began to wear more contemporary clothing which matched the times and their overall line drawings softened to more human like features, and that continual period transformation has continued up to the present. But true vintage Mickey lovers know that it's the pie-eyed Mickey and Minnie (where their eyes are drawn like black oval pies with one wedge cut out) collectors seek out with a fervor, partly because of the uniqueness of the design of this time period and partly because most Disney design purists believe simply that it's better "art."

Toys of the earliest period in Mickey development will have markings such as "Walt E. Disney" or "Walter E. Disney" (and rarely even "W.E. Disney") as the copyright marking notice on the base of a Disney toy. Later, the marketing and licensing division of the Walt Disney Studios became known as Walt Disney Enterprises, so toys from the mid-1930s up until the release of the feature film *Pinocchio* in 1939 will usually have "Walt Disney Ent." or "W.D.Ent." or even the full name "Walt Disney Enterprises" marking the copyright notice on the toy. This marking signifies that a toy is from the mid-1930s through 1939. After 1939, the marketing division and copyright identifications shared the same name as the studio and products are marked "Walt Disney Productions."

The 1930s early Mickey Mouse toys are known for their graphic design beauty, their simplicity, their history, and their tremendous variety. The early Fisher Price toys pictured in this chapter have proven to be such classics that they were recently redesigned and re-packaged as reproductions because their original design was so stunning. Many of the unique Japanese bisques produced in the 1930s were so graphically pleasing and in demand that they were also reproduced and re-packaged in the past 10 or 15 years. But, thankfully, in both cases, the reproductions are tasteful but not exact copies of the original designs so they are not difficult to spot in the marketplace. The fact that anyone would be interested in either selling or reproducing a toy design that is 70 years old bears strong testament to the lasting nature of Disney's original 1930s character designed toys. Among most Disneyana enthusiasts, it's the 1930s toys that are considered most desirable, most valuable, and certainly most rare.

Disney's lasting toy legacy even made some history. In the mid 1930s post-depression era, the Lionel Toy Company was falling upon hard times. As family incomes began to dry up literally overnight during the Depression, there wasn't much expendable money available for toys, even at Christmas. Wind-up trains weren't immune to the poor economy, and so Lionel suffered to the point of near bankruptcy. Add into this story the promise of the Mickey Mouse Lionel Handcar and the Mickey Mouse Lionel Circus Train, and Walt's character merchandising gold mine reportedly saved this American toy company from extinction. Here's a case where character merchandising didn't reflect popular culture history — it made history!

People new to Disneyana collecting might find toy values for 1930s Mickey and Minnie items a bit shocking, but bear in mind that these toys are now over 70 years old and in relatively short supply. As new collectors try to acquire these pristine examples from the golden years they must bear in mind how few newly discovered vintage examples end up in the marketplace. Their rarity drives prices up. But their value is lasting… as good as money in the bank.

As each young child enters a Disney theme park today, and they immediately start surveying all of the current character merchandise available at the parks to be purchased on any given day, they are participating in yet another generation of Disneyana collecting which begins daily. What they decide to buy on that given day determines in all likelihood what will be saved over the next 50 years for later collectors to enjoy.

As long as the parks stay open, and as long as there are children who visit, Disneyana collecting will remain strong. Each click of each turnstile wheel as a child enters signals a new potential collector entering the marketplace, and a future Disneyana collector joins in the hunt.

In the prophetic words of Mrs. Potts in Disney's *Beauty and the Beast*, it's "A tale as old as time!"

Donald Duck 1930s Japanese celluloid windup, 6" tall. $750.00 – 1,100.00.

Mickey Mouse Knickerbocker doll, 1930s, 12" tall. $800.00 – 1,000.00.

Donald Duck 1930s windup nodder, all celluloid, Japan. $900.00 – 1,500.00.

Mickey Mouse windup platform toy, 1930s, Japan. $1,200.00 – 2,000.00.

Mickey Mouse celluloid nodder windup toy, Japan, 1930s, rare. $1,500.00 – 2,200.00.

Mickey Mouse 1930s Ohio Art shovel. $300.00 – 450.00.

Mickey Mouse Marks Brothers of Boston target board, 1930s. $125.00 – 200.00.

Mickey Mouse Hoopla Game by Marks Brothers, 1930s, rare. $800.00 – 1,200.00.

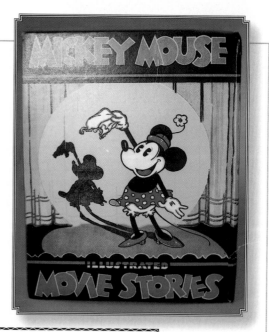

Mickey Mouse Movie Stories book, Canadian, 1930s, rare. $350.00 – 600.00.

Mickey Mouse Marks Brothers of Boston Soldier Set with gun. $550.00 – 900.00.

Mickey Mouse pull toy, 1930s, by N. N. Hill Brass. $600.00 – 1,000.00.

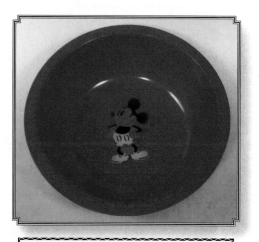

Mickey Mouse Beetleware plastic bowl, 1930s. $65.00 – 100.00.

Mickey Mouse Ohio Art 1930s sand pail. $700.00 – 1,000.00.

Mickey Mouse "Treasure Island" sand pail, Ohio Art, 1930s. $500.00 – 750.00.

Mickey Mouse Steiff doll, 7" tall, Germany. $1,200.00 – 2,000.00.

Donald Duck 1930s windup, 6" tall. $750.00 – 1,100.00.

Mickey and Minnie Mouse Lionel Hand Car, 1930s, with box. $1,000.00 – 1,700.00.

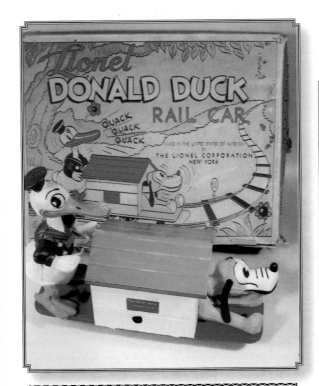

Donald Duck and Pluto Lionel Rail Car, 1930s, with box. $1,200.00 – 2,000.00.

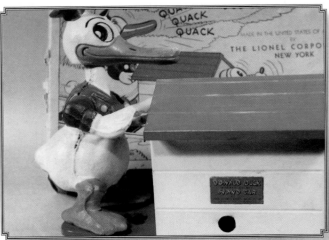

Closeup detail of Donald Duck and Pluto Rail Car.

Mickey Mouse 1930s Japanese celluloid figure, jointed, 5". $500.00 – 900.00.

Mickey Mouse 6" bisque figure, 1930s. $500.00 – 800.00.
Mickey Mouse cardboard figure, 1930s. $50.00 – 75.00.
Mickey Mouse wooden toy wagon, 1930s. $400.00 – 700.00.

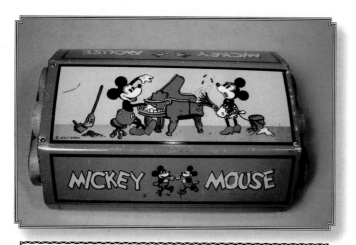

Mickey Mouse early and rare sweeper (no handle shown). $500.00 – 750.00.

Mickey Mouse Patriot China/Salem China child's plate, 1930s. $125.00 – 200.00.

Minnie Mouse Patriot China child's ceramic cup, 1930s. $75.00 – 150.00.

Ohio Art Mickey and Minnie Mouse 1930s tea tray. $150.00 – 250.00.

Detail of tea tray.

Mickey and Minnie Mouse large 1930s tea set, Ohio Art. $600.00 – 900.00.

Detail of tea set.

Mickey and Minnie Mouse horn, tall version, Marks Brothers. $200.00 – 300.00.

Mickey Mouse character blocks by Halsam, 1930s. $300.00 – 450.00.

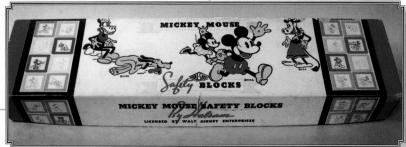

"Double Donald" bisque toothbrush holder, 1930s, Japan. $375.00 – 500.00.

Mickey Mouse jointed celluloid doll, Japan, 1930s, rare, 7". $1,000.00 – 1,750.00.

Minnie Mouse jointed celluloid doll, Japan, 6", 1930s. $750.00 – 1,000.00.

Mickey and Minnie Mouse Yarn Sewing Set manufactured by Marks Brothers of Boston in 1930s, complete with sewing cards. $750.00 – 1,000.00.

Interior detail of Yarn Sewing Set.

Mickey and Minnie Mouse salt, pepper, and sugar bowl, rare. $1,000.00 – 1,500.00.

Mickey Mouse (bulbous nose) 1930s bisque figure, Japan. $250.00 – 400.00.

Mickey Mouse (bulbous nose) 1930s bisque figure, Japan. $250.00 – 400.00.

Mickey and Minnie Mouse 1930s Ohio Art drum, tin, lithographed. $600.00 – 950.00.

Donald Duck 12" Knickerbocker jointed doll, compostion, 1930s. $1,500.00 – 2,000.00.

Mickey Mouse jointed wood and composition 1930s doll, rare. $1,700.00 – 2,200.00.

Mickey Mouse jointed wood doll, even rarer yellow version. $2,000.00 – 2,500.00.

Mickey Mouse Knickerbocker 1930s cowboy doll with tag, extremely rare and in near mint condition. $2,000.00 – 3,000.00.

Mickey and Minnie Mouse celluloid windup trapeze, Japan. $1,000.00 – 1,700.00.

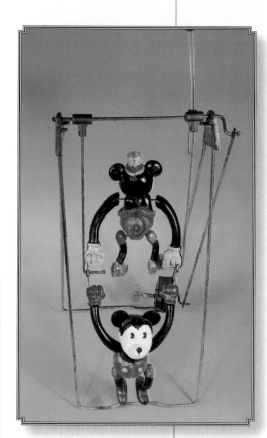

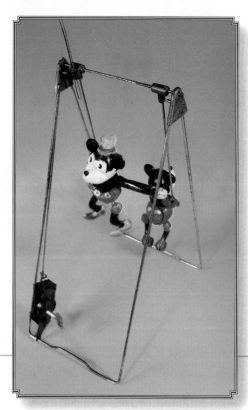

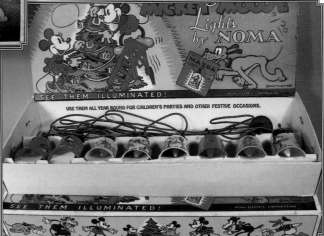

Mickey Mouse Christmas Lights
by NOMA, 1930s. $400.00 – 650.00.

Mickey Mouse palm puzzle by Marks Brothers, 1930s. $150.00 – 300.00.

Mickey Mouse pull toy, Fisher Price, 1930s. $350.00 – 600.00.

Detail of Mickey Mouse pull toy.

Mickey Mouse wood composition radio, 1930s, by Emerson. $1,200.00 – 1,800.00.

Mickey Mouse 1930s child's lunchbox, all metal, rare. $1,000.00 – 1,500.00.

Mickey Mouse 1930s coloring book, die-cut top edge. $150.00 – 250.00.

Mickey Mouse Fire Brigade 1930s book with dust jacket. $300.00 – 450.00.

Mickey Mouse *The Story of Mickey Mouse* big big book. $200.00 – 350.00.

Donald Duck Sieberling Latex Products rubber squeak toy, 1930s. $250.00 – 350.00.

Mickey Mouse 1930s tin top, large 10" in diameter. $250.00 – 400.00.

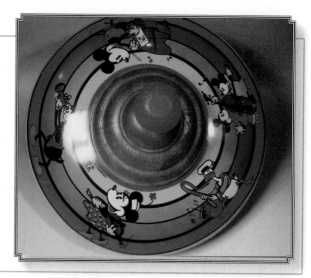

Mickey Mouse large 1930s tin top, 12"
in diameter, rare. $500.00 – 750.00.

Mickey Mouse 1930s boxed
brush and comb set by
Hughes. $200.00 – 350.00.

Mickey Mouse 1930s Fisher
Price drummer pull toy.
$1,200.00 – $1,600.00.

Mickey Mouse 1930s pocket watch with "W.D.Ent." marking, rare. $800.00 – 1,200.00.

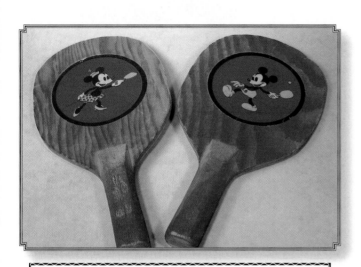

Mickey Mouse 1930s tennis/ping pong paddles. $200.00 – 300.00.

Mickey Mouse Mazda Christmas tree lights, 1930, English. $750.00 – 1,000.00.

Detail of Mickey Mouse Christmas tree lights.

Mickey Mouse Ring Toss Game, 1930s, in box. $500.00 – 700.00.

Minnie Mouse homemade folk art pattern doll, 1930s. $200.00 – 400.00.

Mickey Mouse Fisher Price xylophone player pull toy, 1930s. $400.00 – 650.00.

Mickey and Minnie Mouse cookie tin, 1930s. $250.00 – 350.00.

Mickey Mouse chalk lamp base by Soren-Mangold, 1930s, rare. $1,000.00 – 1,500.00.

Mickey Mouse tin watering can by Ohio Art, 1930s. $500.00 – 750.00.

Long Billed Donald Duck ceramic planter, 1930s, 7" tall. $500.00 – 700.00.

Mickey Mouse soap in box, c. Walt Disney Enterprises. $400.00 – 600.00.

Mickey Mouse jointed wood doll by Knickerbocker, 1930s. $1,000.00 – 1,500.00.

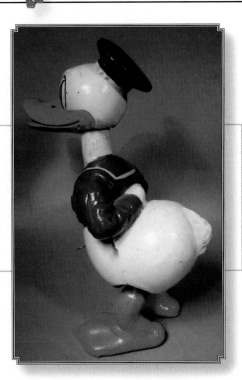

Donald Duck large, 14", wood composition wind-up toy, 1930s. $1,500.00 – 2,200.00.

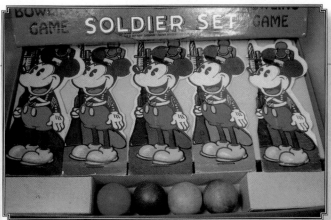

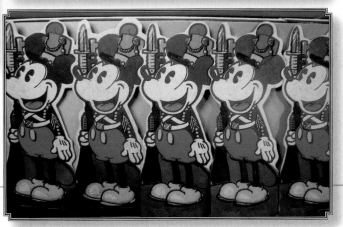

Mickey Mouse Marks Brothers soldier set bowling game. $500.00 – 700.00.

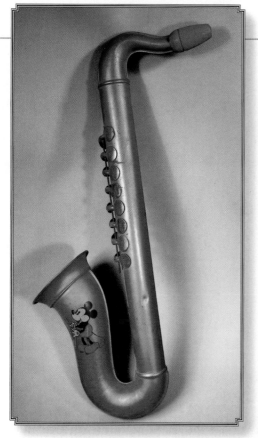

Mickey Mouse 1930s saxophone.
$400.00 – 600.00.

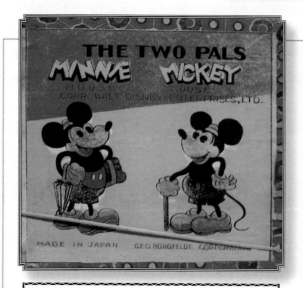

Mickey Mouse "The Two Pals" boxed 1930s bisque set.
$450.00 – 700.00.

Mickey Mouse reverse glass picture for hanging by Reliance Art. $600.00 – 800.00.

Mickey Mouse 1930s Mickey's Garden Sand Pail, pictured above and below, by Ohio Art. $700.00 – $1,000.00.

Mickey Mouse Party Horn by Marks Brothers of Boston, 1930s. $135.00 – 200.00.

Minnie Mouse doll, very rare version by Nifty, 1930s. $1,500.00 – 2,000.00.

Mickey Mouse doll, very rare version by Nifty, 1930s. $1,500.00 – 2,000.00.

Mickey Mouse Book Bank, leatherette case, 1930s. $200.00 – 300.00.

Ad for Mickey Mouse pen set, backed on acid free paper, 1930s. $25.00 – 50.00.

Mickey and Minnie Mouse Piano in original box by Marks Brothers. $2,500.00 – 4,000.00.

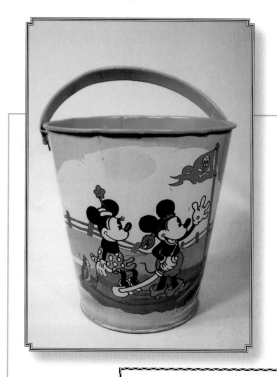

Mickey and Minnie Mouse Ohio Art pail, 1930s. $700.00 – 1,100.00.

Mickey and Minnie Mouse Lionel handcar. $600.00 – 900.00.

Mickey Mouse Toy Lantern Outfit with slides in boxes, 1930s. $600.00 – 1,000.00.

Mickey Mouse giant 1930s waste-basket, rare. $700.00 – 1,000.00.

Mickey Mouse wall night light, 1930s. $650.00 – 900.00.

Donald Duck Sieberling squeak toy, 1930s. $250.00 – 350.00.

Mickey and Minnie Mouse child's tray by Happynak of England. $125.00 – 200.00.

Large Mickey Mouse child's snow shovel, Ohio Art, 1930s, mint. $600.00 – 900.00.

Mickey and Pluto Fisher Price pull toy, 1930s, rare. $1,200.00 – 1,750.00.

Mickey and Minnie Mouse tamborine by Noble and Cooley, 1930s. $200.00 – 300.00.

Mickey Mouse Ohio Art Washing Machine with rare wringer. $800.00 – 1,200.00.

Mickey and Minnie Mouse Ohio Art Washer with wringer. This one has a slightly different paint variety than the machine above. $800.00 – 1,200.00.

Donald Duck Back Up Fisher Price rare wind-up, 1930s. Both sides shown. $2,500.00 – 4,000.00.

Minnie Mouse ceramic ashtray, 1930s, Japan. $250.00 – 400.00.

Mickey Mouse Circus Train engine and stoker, Lionel, 1930s. $700.00 – 1,200.00.

English Wells paper train station for Wells train, 1930s. $200.00 – 300.00.

Mickey Mouse Circus
Train dining car, Lionel,
1930s. $400.00 – 750.00.

Mickey Mouse Circus
Train circus car, Lionel,
1930s. $400.00 – 750.00.

Mickey Mouse Circus Train
band car, Lionel, 1930s.
$400.00 – 750.00.

Mickey Mouse Musicians boxed bisque set, 1930s, Japan. $400.00 – 750.00.

Donald Duck Bandleader Doll by Knickerbocker, 1930s, rare. $1,500.00 – 2,300.00.

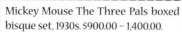

Mickey Mouse The Three Pals boxed bisque set, 1930s. $900.00 – 1,400.00.

Giant 18" tall Mickey Mouse Bandleader doll by Knickerbocker, rare. $2,000.00 – 3,000.00.

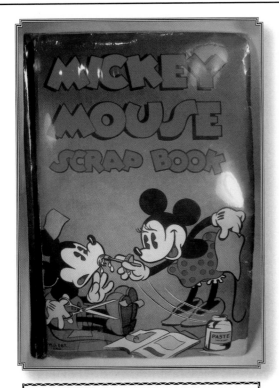

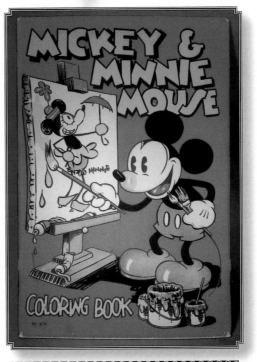

Mickey and Minnie Mouse 1930s Scrap Book (blank pages). $175.00 – 250.00.

Mickey and Minnie Mouse Coloring Book filled with 1930s graphics in full color for coloring examples that are often found framed. $300.00 – 450.00.

Mickey Mouse composition 1930s barker for Lionel train set (pictured on pages 47 and 48). $250.00 – 350.00.

Santa Claus and Mickey figure from Lionel Santa handcar. $200.00 – 350.00.

Mickey Mouse roller skating sand pail, 3" small version. $400.00 – 600.00.

Mickey Mouse Rolatoy celluloid baby toy, 1930s.
$275.00 – 400.00.

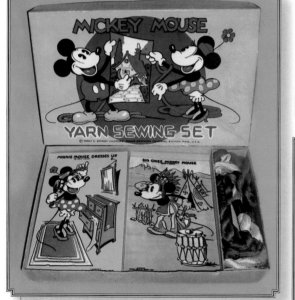

Mickey Mouse Yarn Sewing Set by Marks Brothers,
1930s. $375.00 – 600.00.

Mickey Mouse Chad Valley bagatelle target, English, 1930s. $500.00 – 800.00.

Mickey Mouse 6" tall jointed celluloid doll, Japan, 1930s. $400.00 – 750.00.

Donald Duck 4" accordion player, bisque, Japan, 1930s. $350.00 – 475.00.

Pluto the Pup by Gund, 1930s or 1940s. $275.00 – 400.00.

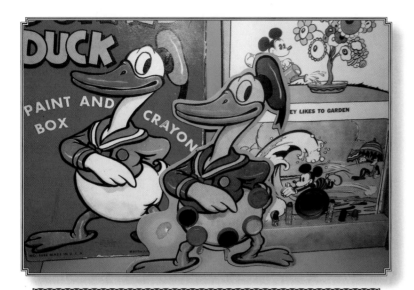

Donald Duck Paint and Crayon Box by Whitman, 1930s. $250.00 – 400.00.

Long-billed Donald Duck jointed celluloid doll, 1930s. $650.00 – 1,000.00.

Donald Duck composition bank, 1930s, by Crown Toy and Novelty. $375.00 – 500.00.

Mickey and Minnie Mouse 1930s bisque toothbrush holder, Japan. $250.00 – 400.00.

Mickey and Minnie Mouse very rare Ohio Art pail, 3" tall. This pail was made for only one year in the 1930s and was originally part of a Mickey fishing set. This is one of very few known to exist. Value is based upon rarity. $2,200.00 – 3,500.00.

Mickey and Minnie Mouse gondolier pail, Ohio Art, 1930s, rare. $1,500.00 – 2,000.00.

Mickey Mouse boxed cube puzzle set by Chad Valley, 1930s. $800.00 – 1,200.00.

Mickey Mouse 1930s Ohio Art tea set in original box, rare. $650.00 – 1,000.00.

Large 12" Mickey Mouse and Minnie Mouse
sand pail, Ohio Art. $800.00 – 1,200.00.

Mickey and Minnie Mouse sand pail, rare
pedestal version, 1930s. $1,000.00 – 1,500.00.

Mickey Mouse and Minnie Mouse tea tray, Ohio Art, 1930s.
$125.00 – 200.00.

Mickey and Minnie Mouse large European tea tray, 1930s.
$300.00 – 450.00.

Mickey Mouse 1930s Marks Brothers tray puzzle.
$200.00 – 300.00.

Mickey Mouse 1930s wood die-cut puzzle, rare.
$300.00 – 400.00.

Mickey Mouse Ohio Art sand sifter with original play molds. $400.00 – 600.00.

Mickey Mouse tiny "Lemonade Stand" Ohio Art pail, 1930s. $300.00 – 450.00.

Mickey Mouse Ohio Art tea tray, rare design, long-billed Donald Duck. $150.00 – 275.00.

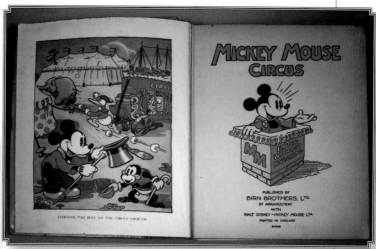

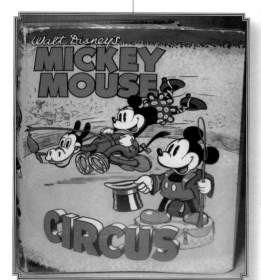

Mickey Mouse Circus 1930s book by Birn Brothers of England. $200.00 – 300.00.

Mickey Mouse Ohio Art drum with sticks, 1930s. $350.00 – 500.00..

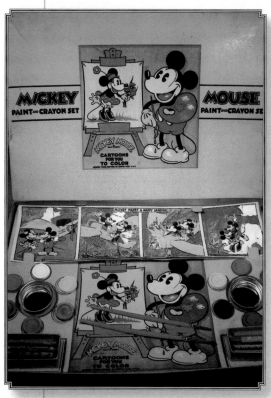

Mickey Mouse Crayon and Paint Set, 1930s, large size, by Marks Bros. $850.00 – 1,100.00.

Minnie Mouse jam jar with rare lid, 1930s, Japan. $600.00 – 850.00.

Mickey and Minnie Mouse beach scene pail, Ohio Art, 1930s. $800.00 – 1,100.00.

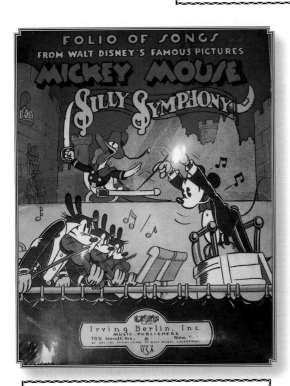

Mickey Mouse 1930s Silly Symphony colorful sheet music. $75.00 – 100.00.

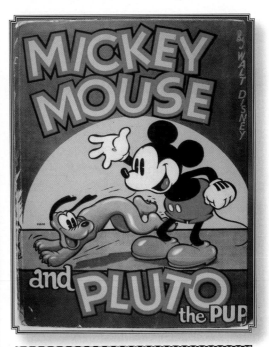

Mickey Mouse and Pluto the Pup children's book, 1930s. $250.00 – 350.00.

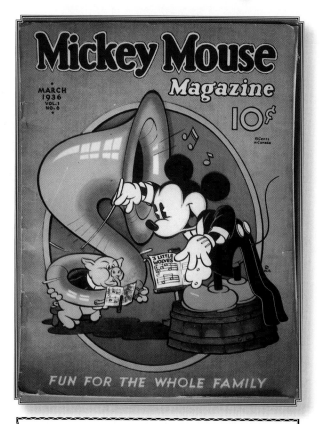

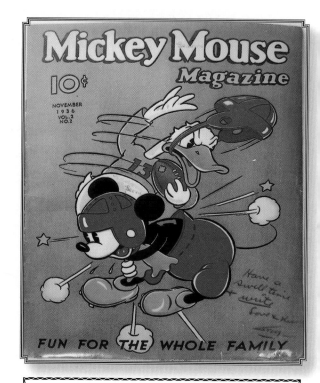

Mickey Mouse Magazine with football theme cover, 1930s. $175.00 – 275.00.

Mickey Mouse Magazine, issued in the 1930s. $175.00 – 275.00.

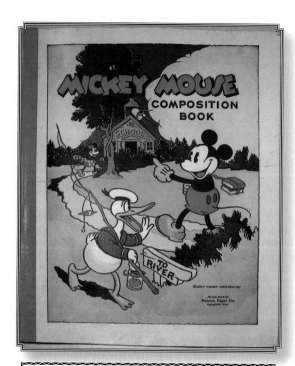

Mickey Mouse and Donald Duck framed book illustration, 1930s. $50.00 – 75.00.

Mickey Mouse 1930s composition book, by Powers Paper. $150.00 – 200.00.

Mickey Mouse Marks Brothers boxed puzzle set (4), 1930s. $475.00 – 600.00.

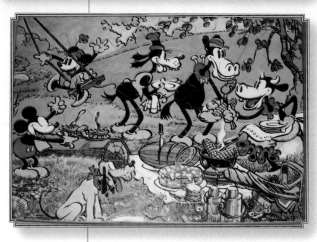

Mickey Mouse, Minnie Mouse, and Donald Duck ceramic toothpick holders (set). $2,000.00 – 2,600.00.

Minnie Mouse toothpick holder, S. Maw and Sons, 1930s. $600.00 – 900.00.

Mickey Mouse toothpick holder, S. Maw and Sons, 1930s. $600.00 – 900.00.

Donald Duck toothpick holder, S. Maw and Sons, 1930s. $700.00 – 1,000.00.

Mickey Mouse on roller skates tin pail, Ohio Art. $400.00 – 600.00.

Mickey Mouse on roller skates tin pail, Ohio Art, variation. $400.00 – 600.00.

Donald Duck and Minnie Mouse sweeper, Ohio Art. $200.00 – 300.00.

Walt Disney's Donald Duck Duet,
by Marx, c. 1946. $1,200.00 – 1,800.00.

Mickey Mouse rare 1930s drum, Noble and Cooley. $550.00 – 800.00.

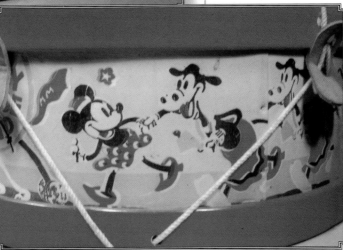

Mickey Mouse bean toss game by Marks Brothers, 1930s. $350.00 – 450.00.

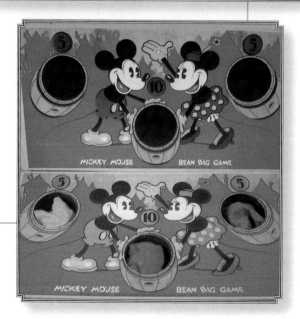

Mickey Mouse and His Horse Tanglefoot, a rare Mickey book from the 1930s. $300.00 – 450.00.

Mickey Mouse Salem China sugar bowl, 1930s. $135.00 – 200.00.

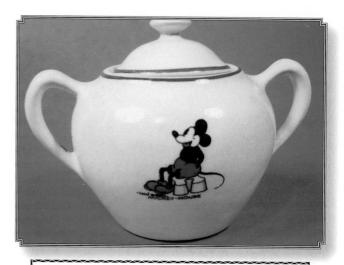

Reverse side of Mickey Mouse Salem China sugar bowl.

Pluto tiny creamer, 1930s. $75.00 – 125.00.
Minnie Mouse tiny teacup, 1930s. $100.00 – 150.00.

Mickey Mouse Lusterware 1930s 4" diameter divided dish (tiny). $30.00 – 65.00.

Mickey, Donald, and Minnie cereal bowl, 1930s, Salem China. $175.00 – 250.00.

Donald Duck and Clara Cluck tray, 1930s, Ohio Art. $125.00 – 200.00.

Minnie Mouse Patriot China plate, manufactured by Salem China. $125.00 – 175.00.

Mickey Mouse Chad Valley Puzzle, England, 1930s, boxed. $300.00 – 450.00.

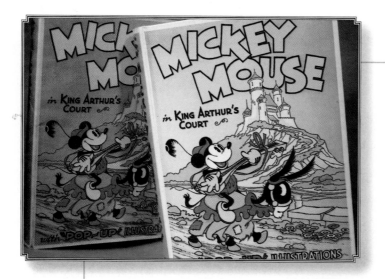

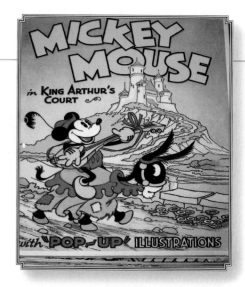

Mickey Mouse in King Arthur's Court pop-up book with original dust jacket. Rarely is this volume found in unused mint condition! $1,000.00 – 1,500.00.

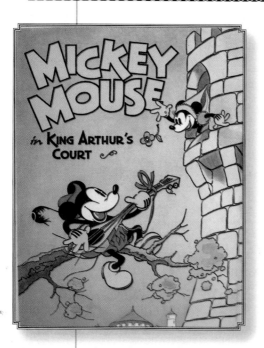

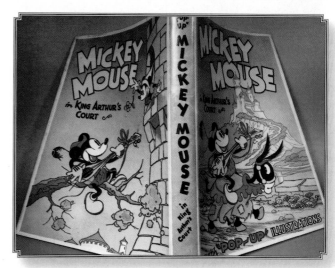

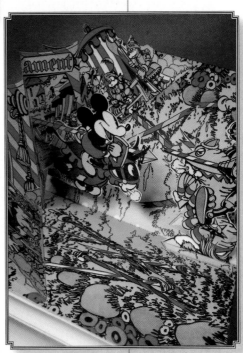

Mickey Mouse Pop-up Book by Blue Ribbon Books, 1930s, $550.00 – 800.00.

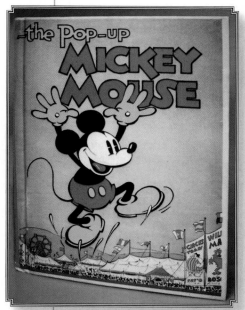

Mickey Mouse Circus Game standup game board. $650.00 – 900.00.

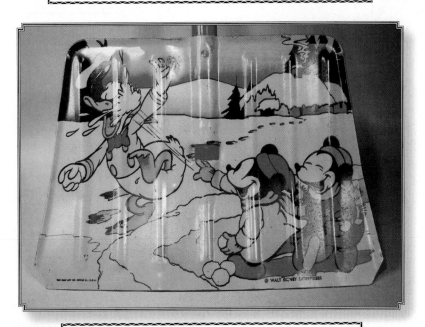

Donald Duck snow shovel, 1930s, by Ohio Art. $650.00 – 900.00.

Mickey Mouse Party Game "Pin the Tail On Mickey,"
Marks Brothers. $135.00 – 200.00.

Balloon Vendor tin wind-up with dangling Mickey toy, rare. $1,500.00 – 2,000.00.

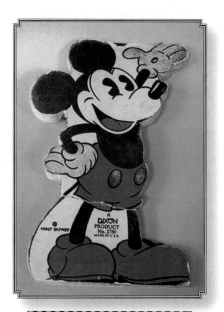

Mickey Mouse paper pencil case
by Dixon, 1930s. $500.00 – 750.00.

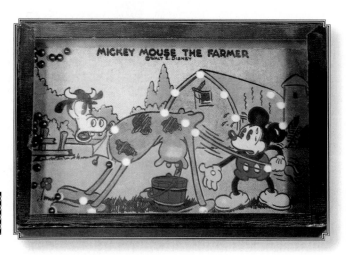

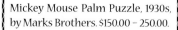

Mickey Mouse Palm Puzzle, 1930s,
by Marks Brothers. $150.00 – 250.00.

Mickey Mouse Tool Chest, 1930s, by Climax. $350.00 – 475.00.

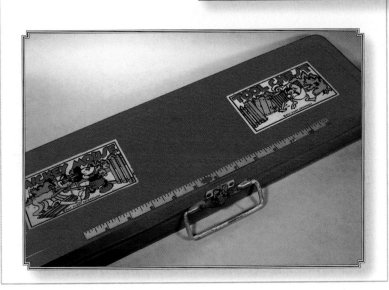

Mickey Mouse Tool Chest by Hamilton of Ohio, metal. $500.00 – 750.00.

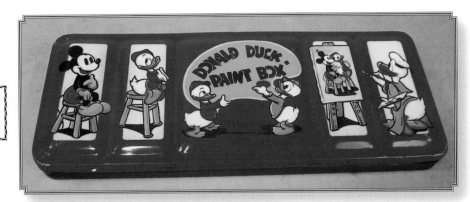

Donald Duck Paint Box, 1930s. $50.00 – 75.00.

Mickey Mouse Treasure Chest leatherette bank, 1930s. $275.00 – 400.00.

Mickey Mouse 1930s Ingersoll box for watch (box only), rare. $250.00 – 350.00.

Mickey Mouse Crown toy bank, wood composition, 1930s. $300.00 – 500.00.

Mickey Mouse Washing Machine by Ohio Art, without wringer. $600.00 – 850.00.

Mickey Mouse Movie Jecktor films in graphic box. $75.00 – 100.00 each.

Mickey Mouse round lithographed tin, 1930s or 1940s, rare. $375.00 – 600.00.

Mickey Mouse fishing pail, large 12" size, 1930s. $650.00 – 1,000.00.

Mickey Mouse beach pail, English, 1930s. $325.00 – 425.00.

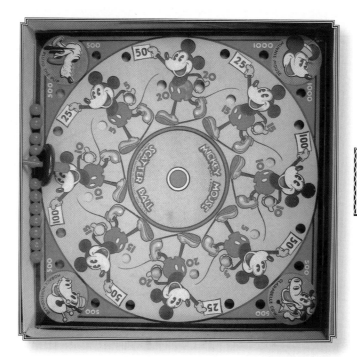

Mickey Mouse Marks Brothers Scatterball Game (interior). $350.00 – 450.00.

Mickey Mouse character top, 8", 1930s. $375.00 – 550.00.

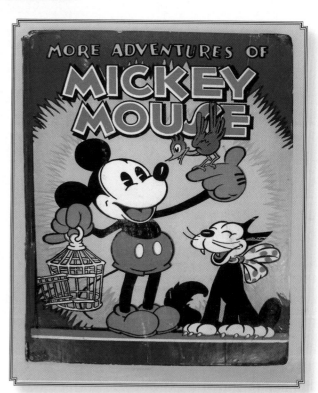

More Adventures of Mickey Mouse book, 1930s. $275.00 – 425.00.

Mickey and Minnie Mouse palm puzzle, Marks Brothers. $150.00 – 250.00.

Mickey Mouse Dominoes Set, 1930s, Halsam. $275.00 – 400.00.

Donald Duck small watering can Ohio Art, 1930s. $200.00 – 300.00.

Mickey Mouse Fireman Patriot China plate and cup, 1930s. Plate, $125.00 – 225.00; cup, $75.00 – 125.00.

Detail of Mickey Fireman plate.

Mickey Mouse on an Island beach pail, 1930s, Ohio Art. $450.00 – 700.00.

Reverse of Mickey Mouse on an Island beach pail.

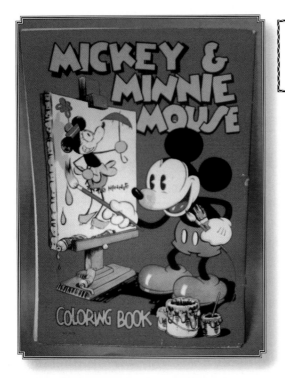

Mickey Mouse Coloring Book, 1930s. $275.00 – 400.00.

Donald Duck composition bank by Crown Toy, 1930s. $275.00 – 400.00.

Long-billed Donald Duck toy, 1930s, fully jointed 3". $200.00 – 350.00.

Donald Duck Crown Toy wood composition bank, 1930s, pink version. $300.00 – 450.00.

Mickey Mouse blocks set by Halsam, 1930s. $275.00 – 450.00.

Donald Duck and Pluto celluloid wind-up, Japan, 1930s, rare.
$1,200.00 – 1,800.00.

Mickey Mouse giant cream pitcher, Japan. $200.00 – 350.00.

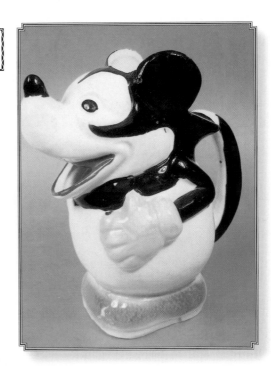

Donald Duck Fisher Price Easter cart, 1930s, rare. $900.00 – 1,200.00.

Donald Duck Beetleware bowl, 1930s. $50.00 – 75.00.

Donald Duck savings bank telephone,
W. D. Enterprises, 1930s. $300.00 – 450.00.

Donald Duck Powers Paper 1930s composition
book. $125.00 – 200.00.

Donald Duck Fisher Price pull toy, 1930s. $700.00 – 900.00.

Three pieces of Donald Duck tea service by Ohio Art, 1930s. $75.00 – 100.00.

Donald Duck tea tray, Ohio Art, 1930s. $75.00 – 100.00.

Mickey Mouse candy candle holders in original box, 1930s. $150.00 – 250.00.

Pluto Modeled in Castile Soap in original box, 1930s. $125.00 – 200.00.

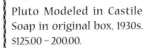

Mickey Mouse Coming Home Game, Marks Brothers, 1930s. $250.00 – 400.00.

Mickey Mouse Magazine, rare Christmas issue, 1930s. $500.00 – 700.00.

Mickey Mouse Ohio Art snow shovel, 1930s. $700.00 – 1,000.00.

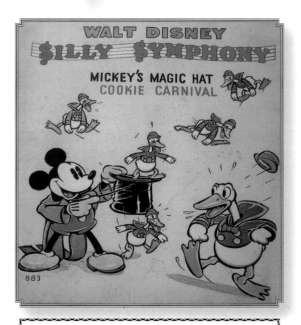

Silly Symphony picture book, 1930s, great cover.
$200.00 – 275.00.

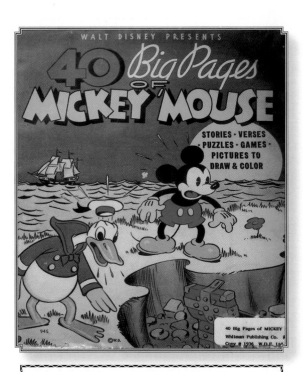

40 Big Pages of Mickey Mouse giant comic book, rare.
$375.00 – 525.00.

Mickey Mouse and Pluto lusterware ashtray,
1930s. $250.00 – 350.00.

Mickey Mouse drummer lusterware ashtray, 1930s.
$200.00 – 325.00.

Mickey Mouse wooden trapeze novelties, by Marks Bros. $100.00 – 125.00 each.

Donald Duck large beach shovel by Ohio Art, 1930s. $250.00 – 375.00.

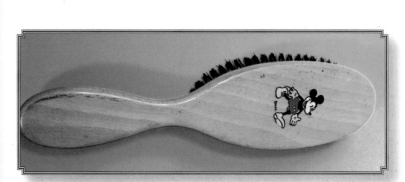

Mickey Mouse character brush by Hughes, 1930s. $35.00 – 65.00.

Mickey Mouse telephone bank toy, 1930s. $300.00 – 450.00.

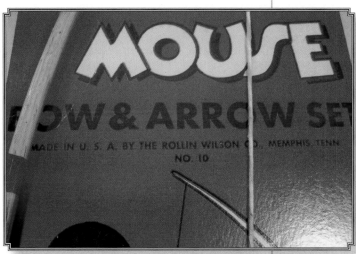

Mickey Mouse Bow and Arrow Set, 1930s, by Rollin Wilson, rare. $600.00 – 900.00.

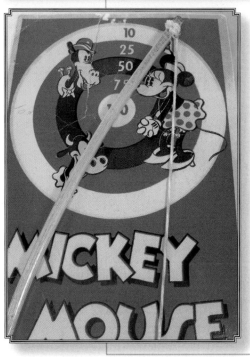

Donald Duck hair or clothes brush by Hughes, 1930s. $50.00 – 75.00.

Donald Duck chalk figure, 1930s. $50.00 – 75.00.

Mickey Mouse Big Little Book, 1930s. $275.00 – 400.00.

Mickey Mouse Sails for Treasure Island Big Little Book, 1930s. $150.00 – 250.00.

Mickey Mouse Post Toasties uncut
character box, 1930s. $150.00 – 200.00.

Pluto push tail wind-up, Marx, 1930s, Walt Disney Enterprises. $300.00 – 475.00.

Pluto rollover wind-up toy, 1930s, Marx. $300.00 – 475.00.

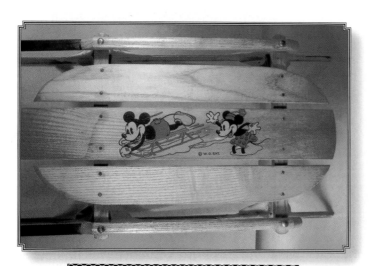

Mickey Mouse 1930s sled, rare. $400.00 – 600.00.

Long-billed Donald Duck rubber figure, Seiberling, 1930s. $200.00 – 375.00.

Long-billed Donald Duck white painted rubber figure, Seiberling. $250.00 – 400.00.

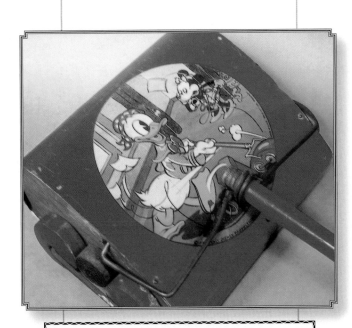

Donald Duck Ohio Art sweeper, lithographed tin, 1930s. $275.00 – 400.00.

Double Donald Duck ceramic ashtray, 1930s, Japan. $300.00 – 475.00.

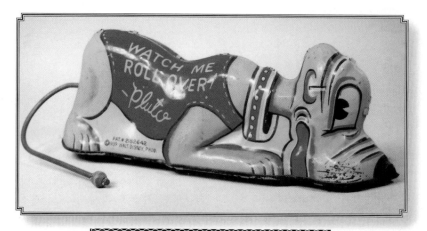

Watch Me Roll Over, Marx, 1930s. $350.00 – 550.00.

Mickey Mouse pencil box, 1930s, by Dixon. $200.00 – 275.00.

Mickey Mouse Beetleware bowl, 1930s. $50.00 – 75.00.

Long-billed Donald Duck English tea set, 1930s. $350.00 – 500.00.

Mickey Mouse Bavarian China pitcher, 1930s. $200.00 – 375.00.

Detail of underside markings on china pitcher.

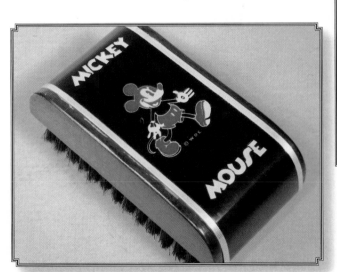

Mickey Mouse clothes brush by Hughes, 1930s. $65.00 – 90.00.

Donald Duck 1930s Watering Can by Ohio Art. $300.00 – 450.00.

Donald Duck 1930s watering can by Ohio Art. $300.00 – 450.00.

Mickey and Minnie Mouse giant 12" sand pail, Ohio Art. $650.00 – 900.00.

Mickey Mouse pull toy by N. N. Hill Brass, 1930s. $700.00 – 900.00.

Detail of pull toy wheel.

Mickey Mouse character doll house, 1930s, large. $500.00 – 800.00.

Donald Duck hankie holder with Mickey and Elmer hankies. $125.00 – 200.00.

Long-billed Donald Duck clothes or hair brush, 1930s. $75.00 – 100.00.

Mickey Mouse large bisque figural toothbrush holder, 1930s. $400.00 – 650.00.

Donald Duck, Mickey, and Minnie Mouse
toothbrush holder, 1930s. $350.00 – 500.00.

Mickey Mouse Christmas cardboard learning aid,
illustration. $200.00 – 350.00.

Mickey Mouse golf-
ers sand pail, Ohio Art,
1930s. $600.00 – 900.00.

Donald Duck beach pail with shovel, 1930s, small. $250.00 – 400.00.

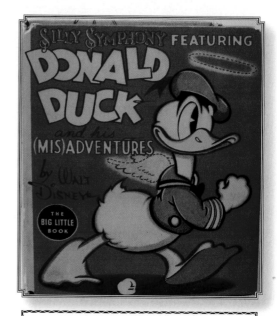

Silly Symphony Featuring Donald Duck Big Little Book, Whitman, 1930s. $75.00 – 125.00.

Donald Duck and Nephews pail, Ohio Art, 1930s. $600.00 – 850.00.

Mickey Mouse and Betty Boop dish, rare, 1930s.
$300.00 – 400.00.

Mickey Mouse English Ring-O-Roses ceramic teapot, 1930s.
$300.00 – 500.00.

Large 10" Mickey Mouse art deco pitcher, 1930s,
French. $500.00 – 650.00.

Reverse of Mickey Mouse art deco pitcher.

Donald Duck large 1930s storybook, full color. $350.00 – 500.00.

Mickey Mouse Pencil Box, 1930s. $125.00 – 200.00.

Mickey Mouse beach pail with original shovel, Ohio Art, 1930s. $400.00 – 700.00.

Mickey Mouse beach pail with original shovel, Ohio Art, 1930s. $400.00 – 700.00.

Donald Duck giant pull toy by Fisher Price (missing front wheels). $250.00 – 400.00.

Mickey Mouse Santa planter by Leeds, 1940s. $150.00 – 250.00.

Mickey Mouse patriot china plate (with Pluto), 1930s. $200.00 – 300.00.

Mickey Mouse Santa planter by Leeds China, different paint style. $150.00 – 250.00.

Mickey Mouse Talkie Jecktor with box, 1930s. $300.00 – 450.00.

Mickey Mouse Talkie Jecktor box.

Mickey and Minnie Mouse Wooden hair brush, 1930s. $75.00 – 125.00.

Mickey and Minnie Mouse tea tray by Happynak, 1930s. $150.00 – 225.00.

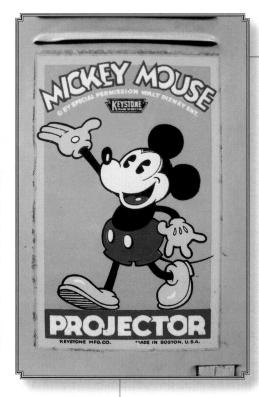

Mickey Mouse Projector, 1930s, by Keystone. $550.00 – 900.00.

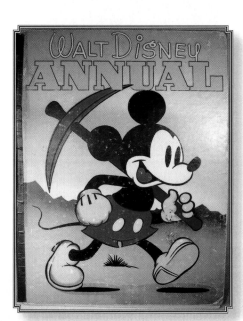

Walt Disney Annual, 1930s, large book. $250.00 – 350.00.

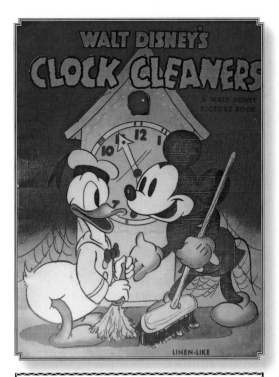

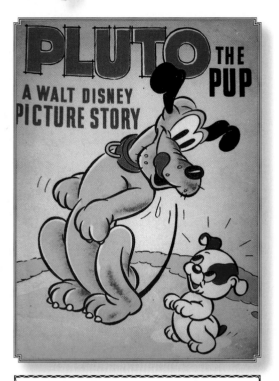

Walt Disney's *Clock Cleaners* linen-like book, 1930s. $250.00 – 400.00.

Pluto the Pup linen-like book, 1930s. $125.00 – 200.00.

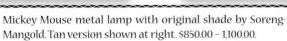

Mickey Mouse metal lamp with original shade by Soreng-Mangold. Tan version shown at right. $850.00 – 1,100.00.

Assortment of Mickey, Donald, and Pluto celluloid pencil sharpeners, 1930s. $90.00 – 135.00 each.

Mickey Mouse 1930s porcelain potty, great graphics! $300.00 – 450.00.

Mickey Mouse pencil case by Dixon, 1930s. Opposite side shown at right. $125.00 – 200.00.

Mickey Mouse Movie Jecktor, 1930s, $500.00 – 850.00.

Three films and boxes for the Mickey Mouse Movie Jecktor.

Detail of graphic on the Mickey Mouse Movie Jecktor.

Mickey Mouse Ingersoll watch in box, leather band, 1930s. $500.00 – 800.00.

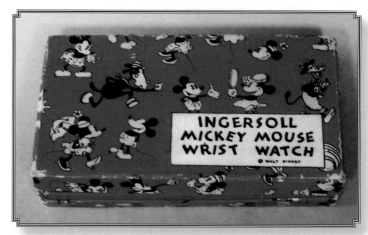

Mickey Mouse Ingersoll watch, box only, no watch, 1930s. $200.00 – 300.00.

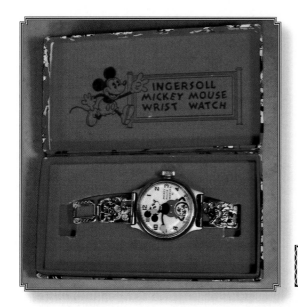

Mickey Mouse Ingersoll watch in box, metal band, 1930s. $550.00 – 850.00.

Mickey Mouse 1930s Ingersoll pocket watch in original box with fob. $700.00 – 1,000.00.

FEATURE FILMS
AND COLLECTING

OST AVID FANS OF MICKEY MOUSE, MINNIE MOUSE, Donald Duck, and the rest of the 1930s gang have a hard time limiting their collecting scope to just the main cartoon film characters. Often, Disneyana collectors branch out into multiple facets of the Disney realm whether it is television inspired characters or those from the feature films. Collectors who focus upon Disney feature film characters are treated to a wonderfully colorful chronology of film characters dating from the early 1930s with the advent of the Walt Disney Studio's releases of *The Silly Symphonies* to the pre-war releases of *Pinocchio* and *Fantasia* with certainly *Snow White and the Seven Dwarfs* holding the honor of being likely the most popular Disney feature film ever produced.

The 1930s feature film toys give evidence of the continued association of the Walt Disney Studios and Kay Kamen alliance. Even though "The Three Little Pigs" was simply marketed as one of *The Silly Symphonies* film featurette series, it is often regarded by Disneyana collectors as a true early feature length film. Kamen and associates found marketing licenses with familiar toy companies such as Parker Brothers and Ohio Art to not only boost Disney Studio profits but enhance the popularity of the entire *Silly Symphony* series including "The Three Little Pigs" themselves.

When *Snow White and the Seven Dwarfs* opened in 1937, it revolutionized the way the world regarded animated films. Prior to *Snow White*, Walt Disney had already introduced the first sound cartoon (*Steamboat Willie* in 1928) and the first full-color cartoon (*Flowers and Trees — A Silly Symphony*). But with the debut of *Snow White and the Seven Dwarfs*, Disney took a leap of faith betting that audiences would pay feature film prices to sit through an evening of only a cartoon. Prior to 1937, animated films were used as short subjects, fillers between full-length features, or longer short subject regarded as featurettes (such as "The Three Little Pigs"). Never before had a film producer attempted to sell to the public a feature-length motion picture animated cartoon. *Snow White's* success put Disney on the map, and won him a very special Academy Award which was presented to him in 1938 by child superstar Shirley Temple. The Oscar featured one large Oscar at the top, and seven tiny stair-stepped Oscars angling down an art deco style stair stepped trophy base. It was a unique Oscar for a most unique accomplishment. Shirley Temple offered an innocent and dramatic line of "Isn't it wonderful, and bright and shiny?" (or something to that effect), as she presented him the award. In photographs of the event, Walt Disney is beaming, proud, and happy, most certainly. The award itself was outstanding. But on that night, Walt was even prouder of the fact that he had not only changed his studio's fortune by validating the notion that audiences would pay to see a full-length cartoon feature. He knew he had changed film history forever.

Collectors will find wonderful doll toy examples inspired by the Disney feature films of the 1930s. Wonderful doll likenesses of all of *Snow White and the Seven Dwarfs* characters were manufactured by Ideal, Knickerbocker, and the Richard Krueger Company in the 1930s. Evidently, 1930s toy producers realized early on that if children were treated to a feature-length cartoon which presented animated characters and heroines as serious stars of the story line, then the kids just wouldn't be able to live without taking a likeness of those characters home with them from the dime store. Certainly Mickey and Minnie Mouse dolls had been widely popular during the first half of the 1930s decade, but the feature-film inspired doll creations were a niche in the toy market that Walt Disney would capitalize upon starting in the 1930s with *Snow White* and *Pinocchio*, and continue for the next 70 years up to the present.

One of the reasons Disney feature film collectibles were available in such a tremendous variety and supply is the fact that Disney really had no competition in the toy marketplace. The studio could only produce one full-length feature every eighteen months to two years, and parents and children knew that if they wanted to experience Disney fun between the releases, they would have to purchase merchandise. Consider the fact that there was no television in the 1930s for children, there was no video or even family home film releases. There was nothing. You saw your Disney friends at the theatre in either film short subjects with Mickey Mouse and the gang on weekends, or watched each new Disney feature that was released every year or so. That was it. If you wanted more Disney, you purchased Disney toys. Eventually, Walt Disney Productions realized that children passed through the feature film age every seven to eight years, so like clockwork and beginning in the 1940s, the studios began to re-release original features on a six- to eight-year cycle. Thus, film greats like *Snow White* and *Pinocchio* could be enjoyed by each new set of youngsters who grew into the prime childhood movie-going age. With the film vault of potential re-releases building and the studio able to release a new animated feature nearly every year, the Walt Disney Studios were able to keep several new releases or re-releases in the theatres at one time. So, by the 1950s, it was rare to find a weekend at the movie theatres when there wasn't some sort of Disney animated feature playing.

Collectors of Disney feature film subjects will find examples in this chapter dealing with first "The Three Little Pigs" followed by *Snow White and the Seven Dwarfs*, *Pinocchio*, *Dumbo*, *Bambi*, *Cinderella*, *Lady and the Tramp*, and several other feature film

character toys. Nearly all were produced with the original release of each film, and all continued to enhance the profits of Walt Disney Productions while at the same time helping to cross promote all the other Disney character merchandise and subsequently released films. The 1930s through the 1950s were a seemingly endless cycle of character merchandising availability and profits.

Of particular note in this chapter is the mint set of Snow White and the Seven Dwarfs character dolls manufactured by Knickerbocker in 1938 complete with all of their beards, original clothes, and wrist hang tags. Other toys worthy of a special look are the extremely rare Emerson Snow White radio, the huge variety of Pinocchio and Jiminy Cricket dolls manufactured by both Ideal Toy and Knickerbocker including a giant 40" tall store display model, an extremely rare plastic Lady and the Tramp platform pull toy, numerous Louis Marx windup toys and a host of unusual family board games devoted to the likes of the many diverse film feature characters released during this time period.

Today's collector has a multitude of specialty possibilities when it comes to collecting Disneyana. Focusing upon favorite feature films and the character merchandise associated with the release of those films is a great way to expand a Disneyana collection beyond the norm of simply collecting Mickey and Minnie Mouse. The nice thing about Disneyana collecting is that no matter how you mix the characters up by theme or chronology, they all look great together because they are, after all, pure Disney.

Elmer the Elephant soap, 1930s. $125.00 – 200.00.

Three Little Pigs bowl, 1930s, Salem China. $125.00 – 175.00.

Little Red Riding Hood and Three Pigs plate, 1930s, Salem China. $150.00 – 225.00.

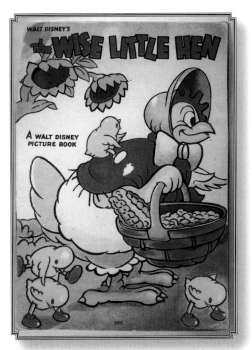

Wise Little Hen linen-like book, 1930s. $125.00 – 175.00.

121

Three Little Pigs divided dish, 1930s, Salem China. $125.00 – 200.00.

Three Pigs and Big Bad Wolf cup, Salem China, 1930s. $125.00 – 175.00.

Practical Pig cup, Salem China, 1930s. $125.00 – 175.00.

Three Little Pigs ceramic ashtray, Japan, 1930s. $200.00 – 300.00.

Three Little Pigs Soap, 1930s. $150.00 – 200.00.

Silly Symphony boxed lamp covers, 1930s. $250.00 – 375.00.

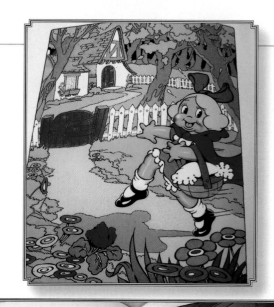

The Big Bad Wolf and Little
Red Riding Hood book, 1930s.
$200.00 – 325.00.

Who's Afraid of the Big Bad Wolf game, 1930s. $250.00 – 400.00.

Three Little Pigs drum, 1930s, Ohio Art, Bryan Ohio. $275.00 – 425.00.

Three Little Pigs wash tub by Ohio Art, 1930s. $250.00 – 350.00.

Three Little Pigs leatherette book bank, 1930s. $125.00 – 200.00.

Three Little Pigs large sand pail, Ohio Art, 1930s. $400.00 – 650.00.

Little Red Riding Hood game, 1930s, rare. $300.00 – 450.00.

Ferdinand the Bull Chinese checkers game, 1930s. $250.00 – 400.00.

Ferdinand the Bull wood composition jointed doll with box, rare. $550.00 – 800.00.

Ferdinand the Bull tin wind-up, 1930s, by Louis Marx. $150.00 – 225.00.

Ferdinand the Bull rubber figure, 1930s, by Seiberling Latex. $125.00 – 150.00.

Ferdinand the Bull composition bank by Crown Toy, 1930s. $200.00 – 350.00.

Ferdinand the Bull pull toy by N. N. Hill Brass, 1930s, rare. $600.00 – 900.00.

Ferdinand the Bull carnival giveaway chalk figure. $75.00 – 100.00.

Ferdinand the Bull carnival giveaway chalk figure. $75.00 – 100.00.

Ferdinand the Bull carnival giveaway chalk figure. $75.00 – 100.00.

Ferdinand the Bull figural soap in box, 1930s. $125.00 – 175.00.

Ferdinand and the Matador tin wind-up, Disney, 1930s, rare. $1,000.00 – 1,400.00.

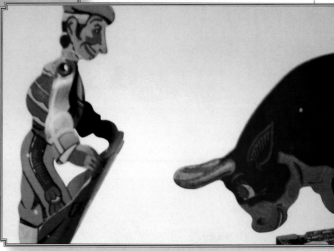

Ferdinand the Bull tin wind-up by Line Mar, rare. $300.00 – 500.00.

Ferdinand the Bull carnival chalk figure, 1930s. $200.00 – 275.00.

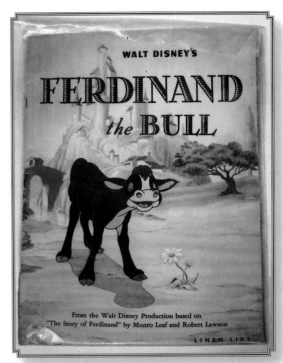

Ferdinand the Bull linen-like colorful storybook, 1930s. $150.00 – 225.00.

Snow White and the Seven Dwarfs Paint Book, 1930s, Walt Disney Enterprises. $150.00 – 225.00.

Snow White and the Seven Dwarfs Paint Book, large, 1938. $200.00 – 300.00.

Snow White and the Seven Dwarfs Big Little Book, 1938. $150.00 – 225.00.

Snow White ad card, European lithography, 1938. $75.00 – 125.00.

Snow White and the Seven Dwarfs pail by Ohio Art, 1938. $450.00 – 700.00.

Snow White mechanical valentines, 1938, W.D. Ent. $50.00 – 75.00 each.

Happy 14" Doll by Richard Kruger, 1938. $400.00 – 650.00.

Snow White and the Seven Dwarfs storybook, 1938, W. D. Ent. $150.00 – 225.00.

Snow White composition doll by Knickerbocker, 1938. $500.00 – 800.00.

Dopey composition doll with tag, 1938, by Knikerbocker. $450.00 – 750.00.

Sneezy composition doll with tag, 1938, by Knickerbocker. $400.00 – 700.00.

Doc composition doll with tag, 1938, by Knickerbocker. $450.00 – 750.00.

Happy composition doll with tag, 1938, by Knickerbocker. $400.00 – 700.00.

Bashful composition doll with tag, 1938, by Knickerbocker. $400.00 – 700.00.

Sleepy composition doll with tag, 1938, by Knickerbocker. $400.00 – 700.00.

Grumpy composition doll with tag, 1938, by Knickerbocker. $400.00 – 700.00.

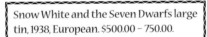
Snow White and the Seven Dwarfs large tin, 1938, European. $500.00 – 750.00.

Snow White and the Seven Dwarfs set of five toothpick holders by S. Maw and Sons, 1938. $2,000.00 – 2,700.00 set.

Bashful. $400.00 – 600.00.

Dopey. $400.00 – 600.00.

Snow White. $600.00 – 800.00.

Doc. $400.00 – 600.00.

Sleepy. $400.00 – 600.00.

Snow White authorized linen-like movie book, 1938. $175.00 – 250.00.

Dopey composition bank, 1938, by Crown Toy and Novelty. $175.00 – 325.00.

Dopey and Doc Fisher Price toy, c. 1938, Walt Disney Ent., rare. $600.00 – 900.00.

Reverse of Dopey and Doc Fisher Price toy.

Snow White small storybook, 1938, W. D. Enterprises. $75.00 – 125.00.

Snow White and the Seven Dwarfs lithographed tin.
$250.00 – 400.00.

Snow White watering can by Ohio Art, c. 1938.
$300.00 – 450.00.

Dopey composition doll in box, mint with tag, 1938.
$500.00 – 800.00.

Snow White and the Seven Dwarfs lithographed tin. $250.00 – 400.00

Snow White and the Seven Dwarfs lithographed tin. $250.00 – 400.00.

Snow White and the Seven Dwarfs Paint Book, 1938. $150.00 – 225.00.

Dopey large ceramic light, 1930s. $300.00 – 450.00.

Happy the Dwarf composition figure (unlicensed, but Disney likeness). $75.00 – 100.00.

Snow White and the Seven Dwarfs safety blocks by Halsam. $250.00 – 375.00.

Snow White Tinkersand Pictures play set, 1938. $200.00 – 300.00.

Snow White and the Seven Dwarfs game, 1939, Milton Bradley. $300.00 – 400.00.

Close-up of Snow White cookie tin.

Snow White cookie tin, lithographed metal, 1938. $300.00 – 450.00.

Snow White hand painted plaster set of 8 figures, 1938. $100.00 – 140.00.

Snow White and the Seven Dwarfs soap with book box, 1938. $150.00 – 200.00.

Snow White and the Seven Dwarfs Target Game, American Toy Works. $350.00 – 500.00.

Dopey tin lithographed wind-up toy by Louis Marx, front and back views, 1938. $500.00 – 750.00.

Snow White and the Seven Dwarfs boxed Seiberling rubber figures. $1,500.00 – 2,500.00.

Happy the Dwarf ceramic cup and saucer, English. $125.00 – 175.00.

Snow White and the Seven Dwarfs boxed bisque set, 1930s. $550.00 – 800.00.

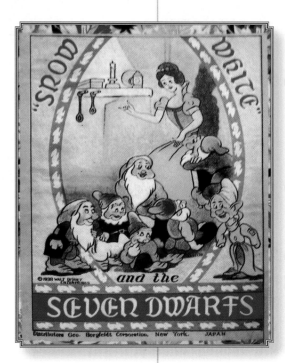

Dopey composition puppet, 1938. $125.00 – 200.00.

Dopey Crown toy bank, wood composition. $175.00 – 325.00.

Snow White and the Seven Dwarfs assorted tea set pieces with tray. $200.00 – 300.00.

Snow White tin lithographed Ohio Art teapot, 1938. $50.00 – 75.00.

Snow White tin lithographed character plate (another view). $25.00 – 50.00.

Snow White tin plate by Ohio Art, 1938. $25.00 – 50.00.

Snow White and the Seven Dwarfs assorted tea set pieces. $200.00 – 300.00.

Snow White milk glass cereal bowl, 1938 premium. $75.00 – 125.00.

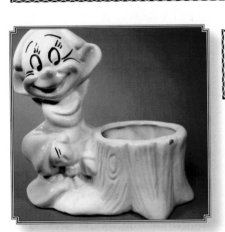

Dopey ceramic planter by Leeds China. $75.00 – 125.00.

Snow White book bag, 1938. $75.00 – 125.00.

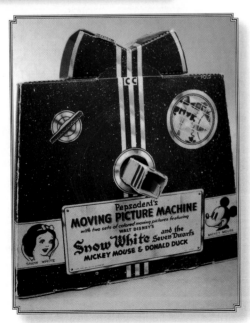

Snow White purse, c. 1938, green leatherette. $100.00 – 150.00.

Snow White Pepsodent Premium Moving Picture Machine. $250.00 – 375.00.

Close-up of Snow White celluloid rattle.

Snow White celluloid rattle, 1938. $150.00 – 225.00.

Happy the Dwarf character soap in box. $125.00 – 175.00.

Snow White and the Seven Dwarfs radio by Emerson. Rare. $1,800.00 – 3,000.00.

Dopey oilcloth doll, probably by Kruger, 1938. $250.00 – 400.00.

Bashful oilcloth doll, probably by Kruger, 1938. $250.00 – 400.00.

Happy oilcloth doll, by Kruger, 1938. $400.00 – 650.00.

Dopey Nite Lite, ceramic, 1938, by LaMode Studios. $350.00 – 500.00.

Snow White compositon doll by Knickerbocker (taller version). $700.00 – 1,000.00.

Doc cloth doll, c. 1938, with plush type beard. $250.00 – 400.00.

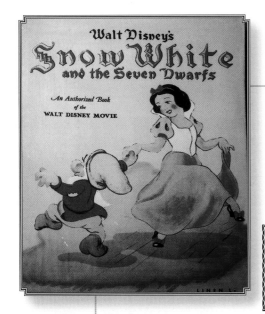

Snow White and the Seven Dwarfs book, 1938, linen-like. $150.00 – 225.00.

Snow White 6" celluloid figural rattle, 1938. $250.00 – 400.00.

Snow White red tin lithographed tray, 1938. $200.00 – 300.00.

Snow White and the Seven Dwarfs game by Parker Brothers, 1938. $250.00 – 400.00.

Snow White figural ceramic lamp by LaMode Studios, 1938. $500.00 – 700.00.

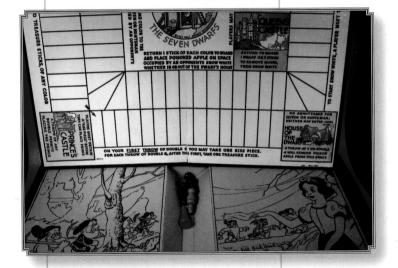

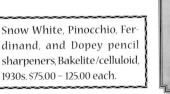

Snow White, Pinocchio, Ferdinand, and Dopey pencil sharpeners, Bakelite/celluloid, 1930s. $75.00 – 125.00 each.

N°12- Pinocchio s'étant enfin décidé à dire la vérité, et de ne pa[s] recommencer, son nez redevient normal, et la Fée Bleue le délivre.-

N°2- La Fée Bleue vient pendant la nuit, accomplir le voeu de Gepetto.-

Pinocchio character post cards, 1930s – 1940s, European. $35.00 – 55.00 each.

N°10- Venant à son secours, la Fée Bleue, veut savoir la cause de son emprisonnement, mais Pinocchio lui raconte des mensonges et voit à sa grande terreur s'allonger son nez.-

N°16- Le vilain garçon Lampwick est changé en âne, à la stupéfaction de Pinocchio, qui persiste à ne pas écouter les bons conseils de sa conscience Jiminy Cricket.-

N°3- La Fée Bleue baptise Jiminy Cricket, en lui disant: "Tu seras dorénavant la conscience de Pinocchio"!

Pinocchio wood and composition jointed doll, by Ideal, 1938. $500.00 – 700.00.

Jiminy Cricket wood compostion jointed doll by Ideal, 1930. $700.00 – 950.00.

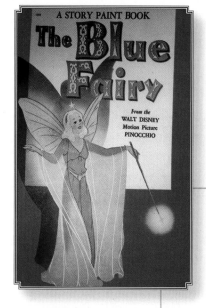

Walt Disney's Pinocchio Books (set of six) 1939, Whitman. $900.00 – 1,200.00.

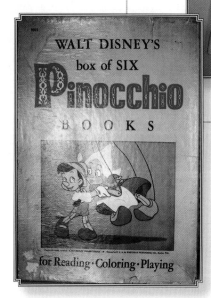

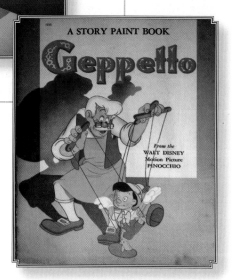

Pinocchio linen-like storybook with full-color illustrations, 1939. $150.00 – 250.00.

Walt Disney's *Pinocchio* small storybook, 1939, $100.00 – 175.00.

Pinocchio's Express pull toy by Fisher Price, 1939. $800.00 – 1,200.00.

Pinocchio School Tablet, c. 1939. $150.00 – 225.00.

Pinocchio Picture Book,
1939 – 1940, with die-cut
cover, front and back
shown. $150.00 – 200.00.

Cut Blue Fairy illustration from a 1930s
Pinocchio Picture Book. $25.00 – 35.00.

This is PINOCCHIO the
little puppet that Geppetto
carved from a block of wood.

Interior illustration from *Pinocchio Picture Book.*

Pinocchio 10" doll, mint with tag, by Knicker-bocker. $500.00 – 800.00.

Pinocchio wood composition doll by Crown Toy, 1939. $300.00 – 450.00.

Pinocchio on the Turtle compostion bank, extremely rare. $750.00 – 1,000.00.

Pinocchio composition bank by Crown Toy, 1939. $300.00 – 450.00.

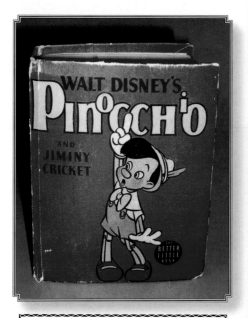

Pinocchio Better Little Book, c. 1939 – 1940, Whitman. $75.00 – 125.00.

Gepetto wood composition doll with jointed arms, Italy, rare. $700.00 – 1,000.00.

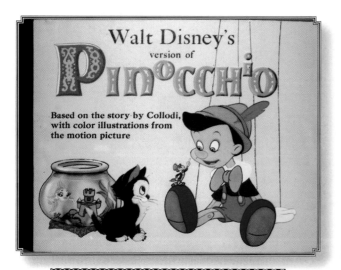

Pinocchio, Walt Disney's Version of, 1939. $125.00 – 200.00.

Pinocchio wood plaque by Multi Wood Products, 1940. $100.00 – 150.00.

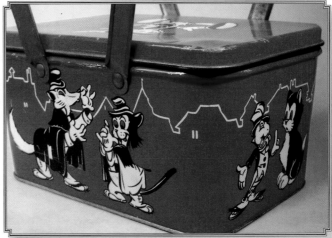

Pinocchio lunch pail, 1939, Walt Disney Productions. $350.00 – 475.00.

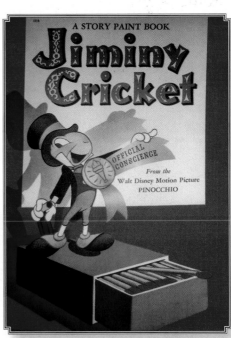

Jiminy Cricket story book, 1939, Whitman. $100.00 – 175.00.

Pinocchio tea tray by Ohio Art, c. 1939. $125.00 – 200.00.

Pinocchio squeak toy by Seiberling Latex, 1940. $100.00 – 140.00.

Pinocchio Pencil Crayons with Wonderful World of Color logo, later issue. $50.00 – 65.00.

Pinocchio Color Box, 1939, with paints inside. $75.00 – 100.00.

Pinocchio cylinder lunch pail, excellent condition, c. 1939. $200.00 – 375.00.

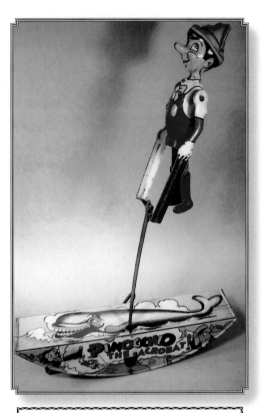

Pinocchio tin lithographed wind-up toy by Louis Marx, c. 1939. $550.00 – 850.00.

Pinocchio the Acrobat tin wind-up toy by Marx, c. 1939. $650.00 – 1,000.00.

Jiminy Cricket tin wind-up toy by Line Mar, later issue. $500.00 – 700.00.

Pinocchio puppet, Crown Toy and Novelty, 1939. $125.00 – 200.00.

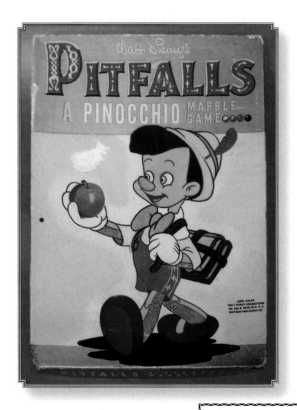

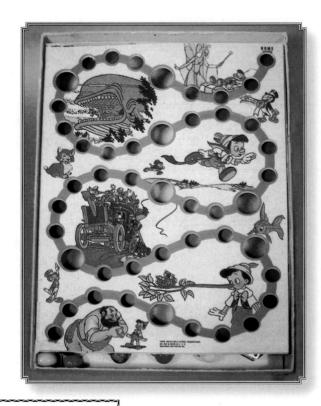

Pitfalls of Pinocchio Marble Game, 1939. $200.00 – 300.00.

Pinocchio doll, Crown Toy and Novelty, 1940. $300.00 – 450.00.

Pinocchio on the Donkey pull toy by Fisher Price, 1939. $400.00 – 650.00.

Pinocchio celluloid baby's rattle, 1939. $150.00 – 250.00.

Pinocchio wood composition figure by Multi Products of Chicago. $150.00 – 200.00.

Gepetto wood composition figure by Multi Products of Chicago. $150.00 – 200.00.

Gepetto wood composition figure by Multi Products. $175.00 – 250.00.

Figaro the Cat wood composition figure by Multi Products. $175.00 – 250.00.

Pinocchio bisque figure, Japan, 1939. $125.00 – 175.00.

Jiminy Cricket wood composition figure, 1940. $300.00 – 400.00.

Pinocchio character fan, 1939. $75.00 – 125.00.

Pinocchio very tall wood composition figure, Multi Product, 7". $300.00 – 400.00.

Jiminy Cricket wood composition figure by Multi Products. $250.00 – 375.00.

Pinocchio wood composition figure, 1939. $150.00 – 200.00.

Giddy the Cat from Pinocchio wood composition figure. $125.00 – 175.00.

Pinocchio character alarm clock by Bayard, France. $300.00 – 450.00.

Lampwick from Pinocchio wood composition character, 1940. $125.00 – 175.00.

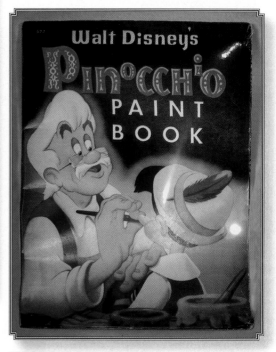

Giant 38" tall Pinocchio store display, jointed, by Knickerbocker. $1000.00 – 1,600.00. Small 10" Pinocchio shown for relative size.

Pinocchio Paint Book, Whitman, 1939. $100.00 – 150.00.

Pinocchio carnival chalk figure, 1939. $75.00 – 100.00.

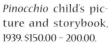

Pinocchio child's picture and storybook, 1939. $150.00 – 200.00.

Jiminy Cricket composition doll by Knickerbocker, front and back. $800.00 – 1,000.00.

Pinocchio Race Game by Chad Valley, English, 1939. $200.00 – 350.00.

Pinocchio stiff cover picture book, c. 1939. $200.00 – 275.00.

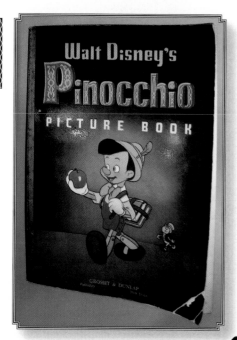

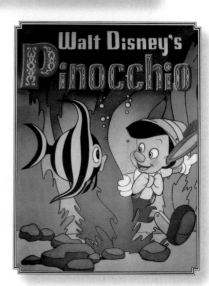

Pinocchio book, 1939, illustrated. $75.00 – 100.00.

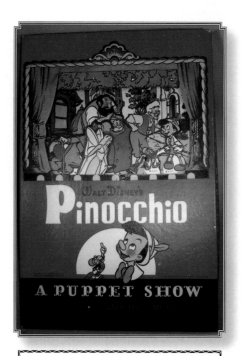

Pinocchio 12" wood composition jointed doll, c. 1939. $350.00 – 475.00.

Pinocchio 12" doll by Ideal, 1939. $350.00 – 475.00.
Pinocchio 30" doll by Ideal, 1939. $1,000.00 – 1,500.00.
Pinocchio 10" doll by Ideal, 1939. $300.00 – 450.00.

Pinocchio Puppet Show boxed set, 1939, rare. $350.00 – 500.00.

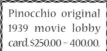

Pinocchio original 1939 movie lobby card. $250.00 – 400.00.

Pinocchio 14" wood composition jointed doll by Knickerbocker. $500.00 – 750.00.

Pinocchio lobby card from re-release in 1954. $75.00 – 125.00.

Pinocchio character post card, European, 1930s – 1940s. $35.00 – 55.00.

Pinocchio, Ideal 9", mint in box, 1940. $550.00 – 750.00.

Pinocchio ring toss wooden hand-held game, 1940.
$135.00 – 200.00.

Figaro wind-up from Walt Disney's Pinocchio, in box.
$400.00 – 650.00.

Pinocchio boxed set of two picture
puzzles, c. 1939. $250.00 – 350.00.

Mickey Mouse Library of Games, complete set. $250.00 – 350.00.

Joe Carioca composition wind-up toy, rare. $400.00 – 650.00.

Bambi by Steiff, 1940s, with original tag. $350.00 – 450.00.

Joe Carioca American Pottery ceramic figure. $175.00 – 350.00.

Panchito rooster character pencil sharpener. $65.00 – 100.00.
Joe Carioca parrot pencil sharpener. $65.00 – 100.00.

Bambi ceramic milk pitcher, 1940s.
$200.00 – 300.00.

Bambi by Steiff, average condition without original tag.
$150.00 – 250.00.

Flower the Skunk vinyl night light, 1950s. $50.00 – 75.00.

Bambi storybook lamp with original shade.
$125.00 – 175.00.

Bambi ceramic plate by Beswick , 1940s. $125.00 – 175.00.

Bambi knock-off (unlicensed) planter, 1940s. $35.00 – 50.00.

Thumper planter, 1940s, Leeds China. $75.00 – 125.00.

Bambi planter by Leeds, 1940s. $65.00 – 110.00.

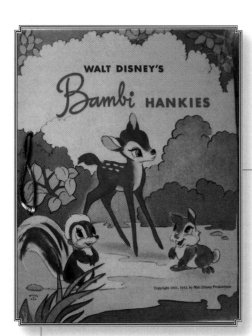

Bambi Hankies book, 1940s. $125.00 – 165.00.

Dumbo salt and pepper shakers by Leeds China, large size, 1940s. $45.00 – 75.00.

Dumbo large pitcher by Leeds, 1940s. $150.00 – 225.00.

Dumbo salt and pepper shakers, smallest size. $35.00 – 65.00.

Dumbo bank by Leeds, 1940s. $125.00 – 175.00.

Dumbo tin wind-up by Marx, 1940s. $400.00 – 650.00.

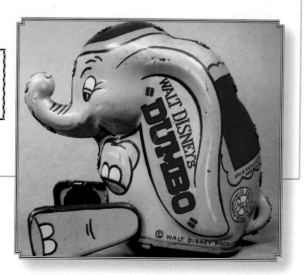

Dumbo song book, 1940s. $65.00 – 100.00.

Lady from Lady and the Tramp plastic pull toy, very rare. $300.00 – 450.00.

Dumbo single salt shaker by Leeds China. $25.00 – 35.00.

Dumbo American Pottery 1940s ceramic figures. $150.00 – 235.00 each.

Lady and the Tramp plastic wallet, 1950s. $25.00 – 35.00.

SATURDAY MATINEES AND THE TELEVISION YEARS 1940 – 1969

FOR COLLECTORS WHO HAVE BEEN LABELED THE "baby boomers," this Disneyana chapter is your own. By the early 1940s, and with only a slight pause in Disney Studio production because of World War II, Disney character merchandising was on a roll. The old relationships with toy manufacturing firms such as Whitman Publishing, Fisher Price, Ohio Art, and Louis Marx and Sons were now moving into their second decade, and dime store shelves were filled with Disney toys during these three decades. This author is a baby boomer, and this period in Disney toy production holds a dear place in my heart.

An interesting question that collectors often raise is "Where did all these toys come from?" It is not a question begging for a factory address or an answer, or even a distribution question. During the "boomer" years, an interesting point of discussion is the memory of how and where we actually purchased our toys. There were no giant toy megastores such as Toys R Us or Children's Palace and even giant discount stores such as K-Mart didn't spring up until the mid-1960s. Most boomers will recount that the majority of their toys came because of two annual events in their life: birthdays and Christmas morning. On the rare occasion that we managed to save up enough of our allowance, then the local Grants Department Store toy department or F. W. Woolworth would be the toy shopping destination. And certainly the wish books produced annually by Sears Roebuck and Company were the inspiration for letters to Santa for nearly two decades.

So this period in Disney toy history could truly be regarded as the dime store years. In the 1950s and 1960s, one of the hottest areas of Disney toy manufacturing was an off-spring company of Louis Marx. At the close of World War II when U.S. ties with Japan were mending, Marx created a company in Japan that produced fantastic toy designs in the likeness of Disney characters under the name of Line Mar Toys. Take a

look at any great tin lithographed Disney toy from these two decades and it is likely a Line Mar toy. Upon close inspection, the trademark for Line Mar is strikingly similar to Marx. It is certain that Marx intended it to be that way. In truth, buyers weren't supposed to notice or even care that a toy was made in Japan. The Line Mar markings clearly read that the toy is "Line Mar," and elsewhere on the lithography would appear the words "made in Japan." But because the two logos used circular designs and both had a crossed "x" pattern in them, a buyer had to look closely and think twice to realize he wasn't buying a standard Louis Marx American-made toy.

Another toy innovation that appears during this period in toy history is plastic. For the first time in toy production, manufacturers moved away from the usage of celluloid for lightweight toys. By the 1940s, modern plastics were being discovered and they quickly became a principal material for toy production since plastic was durable, lightweight, and safer for children to play with. Marx and Line Mar still produced wonderful tin lithographed designs, but paper toys, paper dolls, game sets, play sets and books by Whitman Publishing, and modern plastic playthings quickly replaced the use of tin during this period.

Readers will notice the transformation of Mickey Mouse and Donald Duck during this period. Mickey becomes the "contemporary Mouse Man" reflecting the fashion standards of the day and his image fades from cartoon rodent as it had been in the 1930s to a more rounded, pleasing, and plump well-dressed mouse. Some 1930s purists of cartoon design hate the transformed Mickey. This author doesn't prefer the look, but I live with it. The "new" 1940s and 1950s Mickey is, after all, the Mickey of my own childhood. So he is friendly and familiar. But when it comes to artistic design, I prefer the 1930s mouse. Donald's long bill and feathered upper arms which had been wings gave way in the late 1930s to a similar character transformation.

He was still usually dressed as a sailor, but even he sometimes doffed sporty new clothes in the 1940s. His snout was shortened and his bill became much wider, and most importantly, his two wings became real arms. Animators probably realized very quickly that a Donald Duck with real arms could do a lot more than one drawn with simply flapping wings. And so, the familiar duck transformed, too. Collectors will also find that toys from this period feature the first of Disney's television character tie-ins. *The Mickey Mouse Club* introduced a great line of toys in the 1950s which were manufactured by the new giant in toy manufacturing, Mattel. For the first time in Disney history, with the addition of the singing, acting, and dancing performers who were kids that made up the cast of *The Mickey Mouse Club*, they now had children role models and spokesmen for their marketing on both television and in printed ads. Many toys manufactured in the 1950s and the 1960s bear the logo of *The Mickey Mouse Club* whether the club had any direct connection to the theme of the toy or not. Such things as sets of marbles, chalkboards, drawing sets, guitars and drums, costumes, mouse ear hats, books, and games all were designed with a *Mickey Mouse Club* tie-in.

In addition, the Sunday evening *Walt Disney's Wonderful World of Color* gave rise to yet another wave of Disney toy marketing in the 1960s. Children who grew up slightly later than that period will probably not recognize the significance of the title. Yes, the show was all about the multitude of colorful subjects that the Disney Studio could bring to us regarding adventure oriented nature films, animated features, live action features, and short cartoons. But the "color" in the title referred to the cross-over marketing genius of labeling a national network television program as one that was indeed broadcast in color, as in intended for the family's color television whether a family owned one yet or not. The first five years of the show I watched on our family's black and white television. It was still a great show, because I didn't know the difference. In 1966, we got our first console color television set, and then I discovered what I had been missing. The color was amazing! (And to this day I am eternally grateful that the *Wonderful World of Color* actively showed re-runs. I was able to do six years of catching up rather quickly!)

So, as readers scan the pages of the toys in this chapter, bear in mind that they came to us mainly on birthdays and Christmas, and upon rare occasions, we purchased them with our life savings and allowances. But with each purchase of every toy and every memory, we became loyal Disney fans for life. In essence, these toys were hometown Disney souvenirs of each memory that we had which was Disney. Whether it was from *The Mickey Mouse Club, Walt Disney's Wonderful World of Color,* or *Lady and the Tramp,* each toy represented a choice we had made that somehow that character or that Disney show had connected with us. And as collectors, that connection is a bond that has remained with us for decades.

Mickey Mouse crayons in tin box by Transogram. $75.00 – 125.00.

Donald Duck ceramic figure by Leeds China, 1940s. $75.00 – 125.00.

Mickey Mouse ceramic bank by Leeds China, 1940s. $75.00 – 125.00.

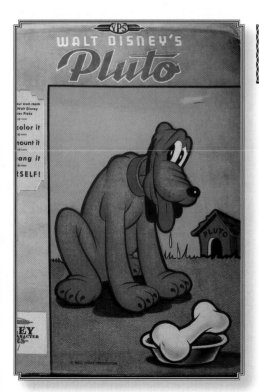

Walt Disney's Pluto picture making set. $75.00 – 100.00.

Walt Disney's Donald Duck picture making set. $75.00 – 100.00.

Mickey Mouse alarm clock,
1940s. $300.00 – 425.00.

Donald Duck giant doll by Lars of
Italy. $650.00 – 1,000.00.

Mickey Mouse crayons in tin box by
Transogram. $75.00 – 125.00.

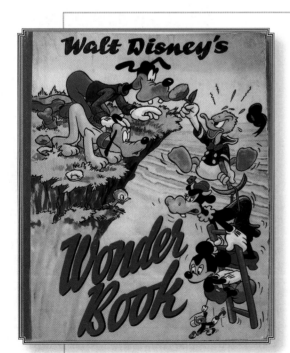

Walt Disney Wonder Book, 1940s storybook, $75.00 – 95.00.

Donald Duck puppet, 1950s. $40.00 – 70.00.

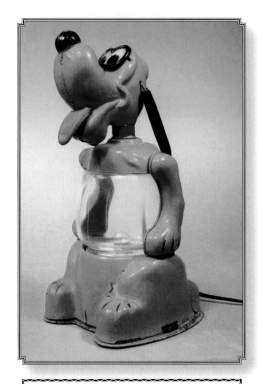

Pluto alarm clock by Bayard, 1960s, French. $350.00 – 475.00.

Pluto lantern, by Line Mar Toys, Japan. $150.00 – 225.00.

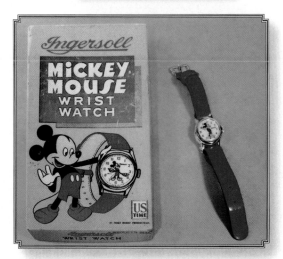

Mickey Mouse Ingersoll 1940s watch in box. $325.00 – 425.00.

Mickey Mouse pair of salt and pepper shakers by Leeds China. $75.00 – 125.00.

Donald Duck hard rubber car by Sun Rubber. $75.00 – 125.00.

Minnie Mouse 1950s marionette, wood composition. $75.00 – 125.00.

Disney top Chein, 1950s. $100.00 – 150.00.

Marx tin wind-up Disneyland train. $125.00 – 175.00.

Mickey Mouse J. Chein ferris wheel, large. $350.00 – 500.00.

Donald Duck orange juice, set of six cans. $50.00 – 75.00.

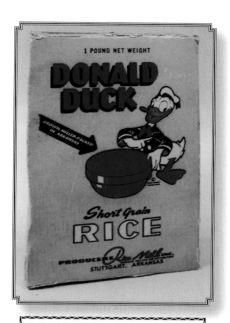

Donald Duck rice in original box. $25.00 – 35.00.

Pluto squeak toy, rubber, 1940s. $25.00 – 45.00.

Pluto jack in the box, maker unknown, 1960s. $50.00 – 75.00.

Cinderella watch in plastic display case. $250.00 – 325.00.

Jiminy Cricket marionette with original strings. $100.00 – 125.00.

Donald Duck the skier, large wind-up in box. $225.00 – 375.00.

Donald Duck hard rubber toy car, 1940s. $75.00 – 125.00.

Jiminy Cricket premium mugs, 1950s. $25.00 – 35.00, each.

Disneykin Play Set from Snow White, 1960s. $125.00 – 175.00. Disneykin TV Stories Set, 1960s. $50.00 – 75.00.

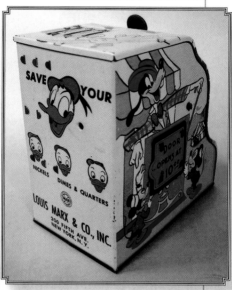

Mickey Mouse large vinyl doll, 1950s. $50.00 – 75.00.

Donald Duck bank by Louis Marx and Co., Inc. $150.00 – 225.00.

Walt Disney's Wonderful World of Color tv tray, 1960s. $45.00 – 70.00.

Mickey Mouse xylophone player, 1950s, tin wind-up. $550.00 – 850.00.

Mickey Mouse Club Newsreel Projector in box, 1950s. $125.00 – 150.00.

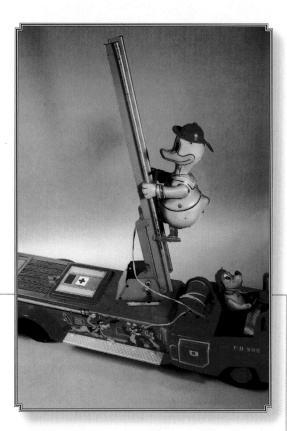

Fire Engine with Donald Duck by Line Mar, battery operated. $500.00 – 750.00.

Dipsey Car original box (box only). $150.00 – 225.00.

Dipsey Car with Donald Duck, tin and plastic wind-up. $550.00 – 700.00.

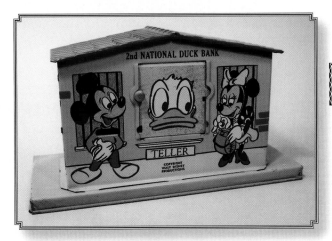

Second National Duck Bank, tin bank, Disney. $275.00 – 400.00.

Reverse side of Second National Duck Bank.

Mickey, Minnie, and Donald plastic walker toys, Marx. $50.00 – 75.00 each.

Donald, Minnie with buggy, Minnie with red dress walkers. $50.00 – 75.00 each.

Jiminy Cricket walker, by Marx. $50.00 – 75.00.

Gym-Toys Acrobats, Line Mar, Pluto with box. $550.00 – 700.00.

Donald Duck and Pluto on motorcycles, tin, friction, Line Mar. $200.00 – 300.00 each.

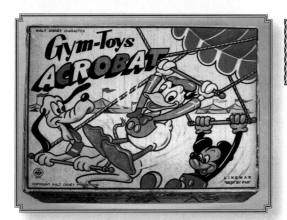

Gym-Toys Acrobats, Line Mar, box only. $250.00 – 300.00.

Gym-Toys Acrobats, Line Mar, Donald with box. $550.00 – 700.00.

Donald Duck Schuco German wind-up toy with box. $600.00 – 850.00.

Goofy Line Mar wind-up, 1960s, Japan. $650.00 – 900.00.

Minnie Mouse Line Mar wind-up, 1960s, Japan. $750.00 – 950.00.

Mickey Mouse Lamp by Leeds, 1940s. $200.00 – 300.00.

Pinocchio tin wind-up by Line Mar, Japan. $575.00 – 800.00.

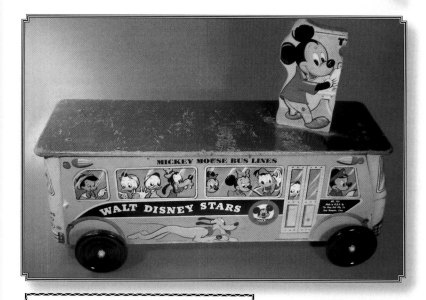

Mickey Mouse Walt Disney Stars bus, 1950s. $275.00 – 400.00.

Donald Duck Halloween outfit in box, Ben Cooper. $25.00 – 50.00.

Donald Duck large orange juice can. $50.00 – 75.00.

Mickey Mouse Puddle Jumper by Fisher Price. $150.00 – 225.00.

Donald Duck Choo Choo by Fisher Price. $300.00 – 400.00.

Disney Rollercoaster by J. Chein, 1950s. $400.00 – 600.00.

Ludwig Von Drake pull-back wind-up go cart, 1960s. $250.00 – 400.00.

Mickey Mouse Sun Rubber airplane, 1940s. $75.00 – 125.00.

Ludwig Von Drake giant 1960s cookie jar. $200.00 – 350.00.

Walt Disney's Television Car by Marx in original box. $450.00 – 700.00.

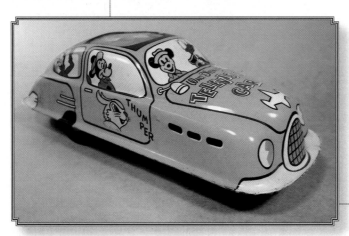

Mickey Mouse Sun Rubber tractor, 1940s. $75.00 – 125.00.

Mickey Mouse Sun Rubber fire truck, 1940s. $75.00 – 125.00.

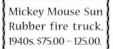

Ludwig Von Drake set of three salt and pepper shakers. $75.00 – 125.00.

Mickey Mouse wind-up car, Marx, 1950s. $275.00 – 450.00.

Donald Duck wind-up car, Marx, 1950s. $275.00 – 450.00.

Lithographed character globe, 1950s. $200.00 – 375.00

Set of five assorted Disney character hats, 1950s. $50.00 – 75.00.

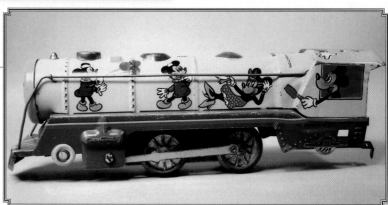

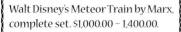

Walt Disney's Meteor Train by Marx, complete set. $1,000.00 – 1,400.00.

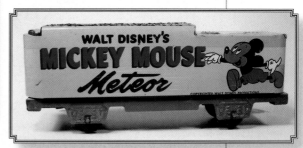

Donald and Nephews wind-up, Marx, plastic. $275.00 – 400.00.

Donald Duck drinking straws, 1950s. $45.00 – 75.00.

Ludwig Von Drake tin wind-up walker, Line Mar. $400.00 – 650.00.

Donald Duck grapefruit juice, unopened, 1950s. $25.00 – 50.00.

Donald Duck canned popcorn with lithographed label. $25.00 – 50.00.

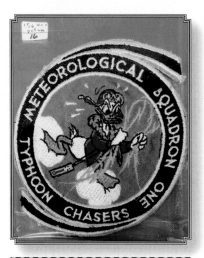

Donald Duck Typhoon Chasers
bomber jacket patch. $45.00 – 80.00.

Donald Duck viewmaster standup ad.
$100.00 – 150.00.

Ludwig Von Drake rubber squeeze
toy, 1960s. $50.00 – 75.00.

Disney's Carousel, rare wind-up, Line Mar.
$1,000.00 – 1,500.00.

Snow White ironing board by Wolverine, 1950s. $75.00 – 100.00.

Donald Duck floating soap Disney squeak toy. $50.00 – 75.00.

Mickey Mouse plush doll, 1950s. $50.00 – 75.00.

Donald Duck western cowboy large plastic bank. $75.00 – 100.00.

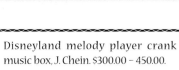

Disneyland melody player crank music box, J. Chein. $300.00 – 450.00.

Donald Duck's Tiddley Winks game, 1950s. $100.00 – 135.00.

Mickey Mouse Sunshine Straws in box. $50.00 – 75.00.

Mickey Mouse top by J. Chein, 1950s. $100.00 – 200.00.

Cinderella and the Prince plastic wind-up in original box. $200.00 – 300.00.

Mickey Mouse Scuffy shoe polish in original box with bottle. $75.00 – 90.00.

Disney's Mouseketeer Television, paper roll player, rare. $400.00 – 675.00.

Donald Duck policeman squeak toy. $50.00 – 75.00.

Donald Duck squeak toy, by Dell. $75.00 – 100.00.

Donald Duck in helmet bank. $50.00 – 75.00.

Pinocchio, 1960s, Colgate's Soakey toy. $35.00 – 70.00.

Mickey Mouse Express Train wind-up toy by Marx. $300.00 – 450.00.

Donald Duck Disneyland tin pail by Ohio Art, 1950s. $150.00 – 250.00.

Mickey Mouse Weather Forecaster in rare original box. $200.00 – 350.00.

Donald Duck rubber play ball by Sun Rubber. $35.00 – 65.00.

Walt Disney School Bus lunch box. $175.00 – 300.00.

Donald Duck salt and pepper shakers, Leeds China. $50.00 – 75.00 pair.

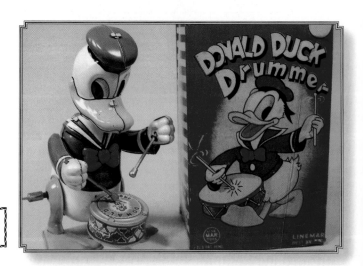

Donald Duck Drummer by LineMar in rare original box. $850.00 – 1,200.00.

Mickey Mouse standing rubber doll, 1950s. $50.00 – 75.00.

Pluto pop-up critter by Fisher Price. $75.00 – 125.00.

Disney jigsaw puzzle in original box. $25.00 – 40.00.

Walt Disney's Piano Book, small piano toy, JayMar. $75.00 – 100.00.

Donald Duck flexible doll dressed as sailor. $45.00 – 75.00.

Donald Duck electric scissors in original box. $200.00 – 300.00.

Disneyland Express wind-up tin train set, 1950s – 1960s. $400.00 – 600.00.

Donald Duck paint box by Transogram. $40.00 – 85.00.

Walt Disney Mary Poppins whirling toy by Marx, 1960s, rare. $400.00 – 600.00.

Marx Disney character car wind-up. $400.00 – 650.00.

RECENT AND MODERN DISNEY COLLECTIBLES

AN INTERESTING POINT OF DISCUSSION REGARDING collecting newer Disneyana is always the subject of debate at antique toy shows and Disney collecting gatherings. How can antique toy collectors justify collecting new Disney? If indeed they are true collectors, then how can purchasing brand new Disney collectibles make any sense since, in truth, they are really becoming purchasers rather than collectors of anything new. Did the original owners of most of the toys pictured in this volume purchase the 1930s through 1960s toys because they were toy collectors? Probably not. So, how can buying recent collectibles (even limited editions) make any real sense?

It is all a matter of taste. Consider first the wonderful Disney Studio creations of collectible figurines manufactured under the line name The Walt Disney Classics Collection. You have seen these in the beautifully lit fancy showcases present at upscale gift stores and in some Hallmark Gold Crown Stores. The figures are pricey, starting at around $50 if it is an introductory membership piece of the year, and on up to nearly $300 if it is a large figure with multiple characters present. Since Disney (and the WDCC as it has come to be known) release many new designs annually, should the true Disney fan and collector jump on this collectibles bandwagon? The figures are stunning, colorful, artistic, high quality, and beautiful. They are the best renditions of Disney characters this author has ever seen, matching the quality of early Disney artists' models which actually aided in the three-dimensional animation of characters at the studio. If I had to make a collectors investment decision for all collectors, I would say they are a definitive buy! Buy these, if your budget can allow it. They are extremely high in quality, good value for the money when the detail and artistry are considered, and they are likely to increase in value since the WDCC continually retires pieces. Once a piece is retired, they just don't manufacture it anymore, and the values usually increase quickly and substantially. So the WDCC annually retires designs and subsequently creates short supply among collectors who missed the piece which in turn creates scarcity and demand. And these drive up the value. Buy these collectibles if they particularly appeal to you and if your collectibles budget can afford it.

If, on the other hand, money is tight and you are first and foremost a lover of the vintage antique Disney toys, buy that which is old. The value of vintage Disneyana never goes away...it adjusts and recovers sometimes, but the value never goes away. Is a WDCC character piece which was retired two years ago more rare than a hard to find 1930s Disney character windup? No. One is a true rarity, the other is a perceived rarity. If vintage Disneyana is your true passion, stick with it. If filling your house with everything Disney is your goal, then by all means buy everything you see that you can afford.

Now, any recent volume devoted to Disneyana collecting has to address the Disney pin trading phenomenon. Bear in mind my label regarding it, it is truly a "phenomenon." The jury is still out on where this avenue of Disney collecting is headed. Readers of this volume will find a very brief sample of what this author does with his Disney pins. I take them off the velvety display cards and frame them in themed collages that adorn my workplace office. I have about 150 students who pass through or by my office daily, and they are all very aware of my pin collections which hang on the wall. They are fascinated by them, but they haven't caught onto the craze yet. This tells me that this is not a national fad yet, but one that you "catch" or a taste that you acquire as you visit the theme parks.

Here's how it works. You visit a park, you buy a lanyard set. That means, you pick out a sort of cloth hanging necklace that will hold your pins you wish to trade or display. One side of the lanyard means "for display only" and another side means "pins for trade." Disney has strict rules for pin trading. No money among collectors is ever supposed to change hands (a fascinating concept for even Disney)! You see a pin you like worn by somebody else in the parks, you approach them and ask if they want to trade. They look over your own lanyard and decide to accept or decline. Simple as that. What pin trading does do is bring total strangers together in a mutual cooperative effort; you make a new friend. Even Disney employees are encouraged to get into the act...nearly every Disney cast member whether a street vendor or an executive just out for a stroll all wear pin trading lanyards. Disney marketing changes the pins on each employee's lanyard regularly, so collectors are on a virtual treasure hunt each day wondering which very rare, old, or unique pins have been secretly placed upon a random lanyard. It's all a very fascinating concept. I buy pins from feature films that I like, and those that I think just "look neat." I haven't started buying them as an investment (yet) because I am just not exactly sure where this is all heading. The specialized pin stores and stands within the parks are usually crowded, so collectors seem to be buying into the phenomenon in a very big way. There's even the value notion that some pins are PPT (which signifies pins from the mid to early 1990s and in reverse and the initials stand for "pre-pin trading"). So, the antiques of pin trading are those from the early 1990s? That's an odd concept. I saw what happened to the Disney Beanie Baby market when the associated popularity of TY Beanie Babies went bust. The Disney Beanies are still in the

parks today, but there's no line standing there waiting to buy them. That fad is over. As a Disney collector now into his fourth decade of collecting, I will reserve final judgment on pin collecting. The pins are wonderful conversation starters and pin trading has brought new collectors into the Disney fold, and that is always a good thing. I just worry about collectors who tell me that they have 20,000 pins at home in 40 volumes (carrying cases) and they don't see an end in sight. For their sake, I hope there isn't an end. But, in truth, that's a lot of pins!

It's a tough call to make on similar other trends in newer Disneyana collectibles. In the late 1980s and on into the 1990s, original Disney Studio animation art values skyrocketed. Prior to the present age of computer animation where nearly all of the art process is electronic, early film studio releases up through the 1980s still required "cels" to be photographed one at a time in sequence to make the process of film animation work. This meant that actual human beings applied ink and paint to early plastic celluloid sheets, and collectors went wild about owning actual art pieces of Disney Studio releases. (In the the 1950s and 1960s these were actually sold to the public in Disneyland for just several dollars!) When original celluloid examples from the earliest Disney films started approaching the $10,000 mark for a very rare multiple character setup complete with an original background, Disney marketing realized that people were interested in owning "original" Disney art. So, the Disney Gallery stores opened at the theme parks where sericels, not actually used in a film but were produced with ink and paint similar to original cels and sold in limited editions, and true numbered limited editions of cels are marketed to this day in those fine Disney art stores. The art sold here is high quality and gorgeous, but buyers do need to realize that these limited edition cels which can range from several hundred to several thousand dollars are just re-creations of Disney animation art, they are not actual celluloid art created for the photography of film animation. If I had the ability as an author to look into the magic Disney crystal ball and make predictions as to what new collectibles will increase with great value, or at least hold their own, I could triple this book's sales. But I am not a soothsayer. I am just a writer who has pursued this passion for over half of my life. And I hope, in the process, I have learned something about Disney collectible trends. So, here's Dave's buy list. Take it or leave it, but here's where I think you should be putting your newer Disneyana dollars these days:

BUY extremely limited editions of figurines, art, and posters that have editions of 500 or less and are of very high quality. If you want to buy these now, somebody else likely will in the future.

BUY Disney character dolls that have small limited editions and are painfully expensive. If you like the character and the doll design, and can plan to live with your new friend for ten years or more, you have a true investment.

BUY Disney feature film games that don't require batteries! These don't have to be expensive, but their art and design should be outstanding. Board games are stable to store for years (they are made to be used over and over, after all) and they have lasting value. Disney has recently begun to re-release old board games from the 1950s such as the Disneyland Monorail game and these sell briskly in the parks. If Disney has recognized their importance, then avid collectors might take note.

BUY any classic style Disney toy that reflects the timeless nature of a character that comes in a great graphic box. Keep the toy in the box, and preserve the box, too. Original boxes with character art can triple the value of a toy even just ten years down the road. Store these in a dry place.

Okay, that's my list. I have learned some lessons the hard way. When my daughter, Claire, was young, we went after Disney pogs in a big way. Now, who on earth (except a loving father) knows what a pog even was or was used for? I don't. But we must have bought a thousand of them. And my daughter's fascination with them lasted about two weeks. We couldn't even give them away at our annual yard sale two years later! Avoid fads, buy that which is timeless and classic and beautiful. Use your head.

It is this author's hope that both advanced and novice collectors alike will use this book as yet another resource to know what is out there in the Disneyana marketplace to discover at the next toy show, flea market, or online auction sale. Keep your wits about you, buy what you love, and enjoy the people you meet along the way. In actuality, it's more about the people than the toys anyway.

Mickey Mouse jointed 7" figure. $15.00 – 25.00.

Minnie Mouse jointed 7" figure. $15.00 – 25.00.

Mickey and Minnie in boat resin figure. $10.00 – 15.00.

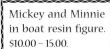

Minnie Mouse 4" 1930s reproduction doll. $10.00 – 15.00.

Mickey Mouse 4" 1930s reproduction doll. $10.00 – 15.00.

Mickey Mouse on hobby horse spring action toy. $10.00 – 20.00.

Mickey Mouse in automobile resin ornament. $5.00 – 15.00.

Mickey Mouse resin bandleader bobble-head. $20.00 – 30.00.

Mickey Mouse Barker figure by Pride Lines, 1990s. $75.00 – 100.00.

Mickey Mouse acrobat on drum resin figure. $20.00 – 30.00.

Mickey and Minnie Mouse hurdy gurdy resin figure. $30.00 – 40.00.

Mickey Mouse plush doll, Disney Store. $20.00 – 40.00.

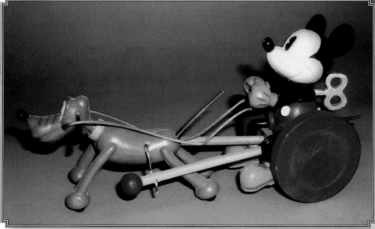

Mickey Mouse simulated wind-up with Pluto resin figure. $40.00 – 50.00.

Mickey Mouse Barn Dance vintage story book. $5.00 – 10.00.

Minnie Mouse plus doll, Disney Store. $20.00 – 40.00.

Donald Duck Saludos Amigos collector plate, 1980s. $25.00 – 35.00.

Mickey and Minnie Mouse treasure bank (reproduction). $20.00 – 30.00.

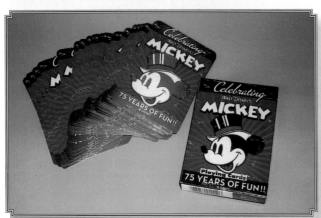

Mickey Mouse vintage design playing cards. $5.00 – 10.00 each.

Donald Duck tin wind-up by Schilling. $15.00 – 25.00.

Long-billed Donald Duck marionette. $100.00 – 150.00.

Goofy candleholder, thought to be from the 1930s, but actually the 1970s. $20.00 – 30.00.

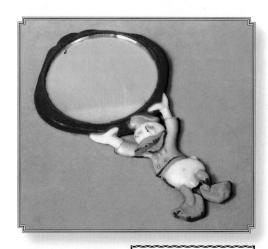

Donald Duck novelty mirror, date unknown. $5.00 – 10.00.

Snow White character soap, 1980s. $10.00 – 15.00.

Mickey Mouse choo choo ornament. $10.00 – 15.00.

Mickey Mouse pocket watch ornament. $10.00 – 15.00.

Mickey Mouse miniature rocking horse ornament. $10.00 – 15.00.

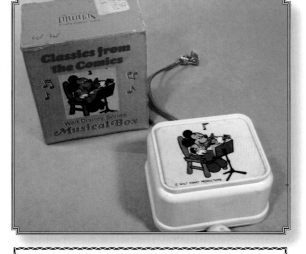

Mickey Mouse boxed musical box for crib. $15.00 – 25.00.

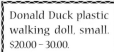

Donald Duck plastic walking doll, small. $20.00 – 30.00.

Mickey Mouse Hardees popup birthday display, open. $20.00 – 30.00.

Mickey and Minnie Mouse tv tray. $20.00 – 30.00.

Mickey Mouse Mouseketeer's hat, 1980s version. $10.00 – 15.00.

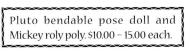

Pluto bendable pose doll and Mickey roly poly. $10.00 – 15.00 each.

Mickey push puppet and Mickey plastic sharpener. $15.00 – 20.00 each.

Jiminy Cricket figure probably by Bully. $10.00 – 15.00. Jiminy Cricket figure in diecast car. $20.00 – 30.00.

Mickey on skiis ornament.
$10.00 – 15.00.

Cinderella, set of seven pins.
$200.00 – 300.00.

Mickey and Minnie Mouse boxed ornament. $5.00 – 10.00.

Little Mermaid, set of 10 pins. $150.00 – 300.00.

Mickey Mouse snow globe.
$25.00 – 35.00.

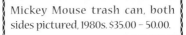

Mickey Mouse comb with saying on it. $5.00 – 7.00.

Mickey Mouse trash can, both sides pictured, 1980s. $35.00 – 50.00.

Mickey Mouse Magazine reproduction art puzzle. $10.00 – 15.00.

Mickey Mouse large 1960s Mousegetar. $40.00 – 70.00.

Disney On Parade tambourine, 1980s. $15.00 – 25.00.

Rabbit plush doll. $20.00 – 30.00.

Mickey Mouse watch in box. $75.00 – 100.00.

Roo plush doll. $10.00 – 20.00.

Finding Nemo character play set. $10.00 – 15.00.

Beauty and the Beast snow globe. $75.00 – 100.00.

Little Mermaid character play set. $10.00 – 15.00.

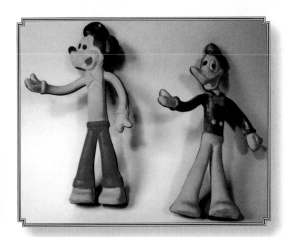

Mickey Mouse and Donald Duck bendable figures. $5.00 – 10.00 each.

The Little Mermaid deluxe multi-globe snowglobe. $90.00 – 110.00.

The Happiest Celebration On Earth giant Disney paperweight. $25.00 – 35.00.

Pair of Mickey and Minnie Mouse heart-shaped ornaments. $10.00 – 20.00.

Mickey Mouse large resin figure that holds small picture. $20.00 – 30.00.

Mickey Mouse alarm clock by Bradley. $50.00 – 65.00.

Limited edition pin set, all four Disney Park castles. $100.00 – 150.00.

Deluxe Ariel, Little Mermaid glamour doll. $75.00 – 125.00.

Barbie as Belle, from Disney's Beauty and the Beast. $50.00 – 100.00.

Tinkerbelle character doll. $45.00 – 90.00.

Beauty and the Beast Belle in ball gown. $75.00 – 125.00.

Alice in Wonderland doll. $45.00 – 90.00.

Tigger small plush child's toy. $10.00 – 20.00.

Sleeping Beauty doll. $65.00 – 90.00.

Tigger, terrycloth plush bean bag toy. $15.00 – 20.00.

Snow White doll. $75.00 – 100.00.

Cinderella doll. $75.00 – 100.00.

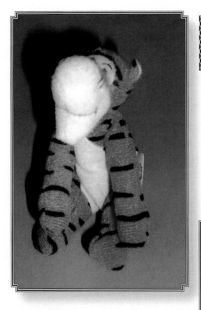

Tigger tiny plush stuffed toy, unusual. $10.00 – 20.00.

Walt Disney's Classics Collection, Pinocchio running figure. $75.00 – 100.00.

Tigger giant ceramic savings bank. $20.00 – 30.00.

Walt Disney's Classics Collection, Blue Fairy figure. $150.00 – 200.00.

Walt Disney's Classics Collection, Jiminy Cricket figure. $65.00 – 90.00.

Walt Disney's Classics Collection, Belle, from Beauty and the Beast. $125.00 – 200.00.

Walt Disney's Classics Collection, Mickey, Fantasia figure. $125.00 – 200.00.

Ariel from The Little Mermaid, WDCC ceramic figure. $125.00 – 200.00.

Mickey on the World, WDCC ceramic figure on acrylic base. $135.00 – 175.00.

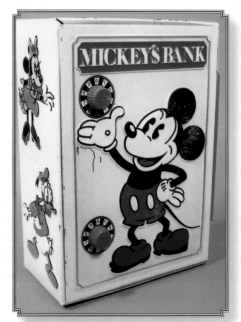

Mickey's Bank, 1930s style tin candy container, 1980s. $15.00 – 20.00.

Master Replicas vintage Disneyland Monorail scale model. $150.00 – 300.00.

Mickey Mouse resin desk clock, 5" tall. $30.00 – 40.00.

Mickey Mouse resin stocking holder. $20.00 – 25.00.

Mickey Mouse organ grinder picture frame. $15.00 – 25.00.

Mickey Mouse fireman resin figure. $10.00 – 15.00.

Mickey Mouse policeman resin figure. $10.00 – 15.00.

Donald Duck in rain-coat ceramic figure. $30.00 – 40.00.

Mickey and Minnie Mouse Schmid music box, 1980s. $50.00 – 75.00.

Mickey Mouse jack in the box, 1960s or 1970s. $75.00 – 125.00.

Mickey Mouse large plush doll. $15.00 – 30.00.

Minnie Mouse large plush doll. $15.00 – 30.00.

Mickey Mouse Riding Pluto vintage reproduction toy. $15.00 – 25.00.

Mickey Mouse vintage style telephone, 1990s. $100.00 – 150.00.

Mickey Mouse Hallmark vintage style ornament. $20.00 – 30.00.

Mickey Mouse riding sled ornament. $15.00 – 20.00.

Christopher Robin Beswick figure. $75.00 – 100.00.

Winnie the Pooh Beswick figure. $75.00 – 100.00.

Tigger ceramic figure. $15.00 – 20.00.

Minnie Mouse small plush toy, vintage style. $15.00 – 25.00.

Mickey Mouse small plush toy, vintage style. $15.00 – 25.00.

Minnie Mouse large vintage style collectible doll. $20.00 – 30.00.

Donald Duck giant 25" resin display figure. $150.00 – 225.00.

Tigger writing on heart collectible figure. $30.00 – 45.00.

Tigger and Pooh small plush figures. $10.00 – 20.00 each.

Mickey Mouse large vintage style collectible doll. $20.00 – 30.00.

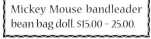

Mickey Mouse reproduction 1930s Bagatelle game. $15.00 – 20.00.

Mickey Mouse giant 25" resin display figure. $150.00 – 225.00.

Mickey Mouse bandleader bean bag doll. $15.00 – 25.00.

Mickey and Minnie Mouse 5" resin figures. $30.00 – 45.00 pair.

Mickey Mouse, 100 Years (Walt Disney's Birthday) snowglobe. $20.00 – 30.00.

Mickey Mouse as Sorcerer bisque figure, large, 7". $25.00 – 30.00.

Donald Duck Mattel Fisher Price reproduction pull toy. $55.00 – 75.00.

Pinocchio bobblehead small paperweight, resin. $10.00 – 20.00.

Mickey Mouse Mattel Fisher Price reproduction pull toy. $55.00 – 75.00.

Mickey Mouse, artist with brush snowglobe. $20.00 – 30.00.

Mickey Mouse Mousegetar Jr. boxed reproduction toy. $50.00 – 75.00.

Long-billed Donald Duck bean bag toy. $15.00 – 20.00.

Mickey Mouse/ Walt Disney World souvenir baseball. $5.00 – 10.00.

Mickey and Minnie animated Christmas display toy. $20.00 – 30.00.

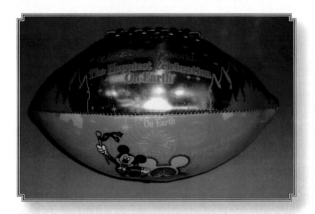

Mickey Mouse /Walt Disney World football. $8.00 – 15.00.

Mickey Mouse vintage reproduction radio. $50.00 – 75.00.

Set of 35 Disney trading pins in special frame, unusual. $200.00 – 400.00.

Mickey Mouse and Minnie Mouse reproduction wind-ups. $25.00 – 40.00 pair.

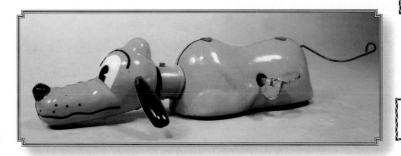

Pluto the Pup reproduction tin wind-up toy. $12.00 – 20.00.

Tinkerbelle limited edition pins set. $75.00 – 100.00.

Little Mermaid limited edition collector pins set. $125.00 – 150.00.

Mickey Mouse as the Sorcerer's Apprentice limited edition pins. $125.00 – 140.00.

Mickey Mouse Brave Little Tailor WDCC figure. $125.00 – 160.00.

Mickey Mouse character desk clock, 1990s. $50.00 – 75.00.

Mickey Mouse salt and peppers from 1980s. $15.00 – 20.00 pair.

Mickey Mouse in tuxedo with cane, acrylic base, WDCC. $85.00 – 140.00.

Mickey Mouse bandleader on special base, WDCC. $125.00 – 175.00.

Mickey Mouse Season's Greeting limited edition pin set. $125.00 – 150.00.

Belle from Beauty and the Beast with sheep limited edition pins. $75.00 – 100.00.

Lion King print with eight character pins from Disney. $140.00 – 175.00.

Peter Pan group of very limited edition pins on map background. $125.00 – 150.00.

COLLECTOR'S GUIDE

THIS CHAPTER IS INTENDED TO BE AN AID FOR TOY collectors of all ages and levels who might need a little additional information in regard to maintaining a toy collection and expanding it. There are really two parts to this chapter. Part one deals with toy maintenance and preservation and part two deals with expanding your collection. Even though this author has been a writer for many toy publications over the past 30 years, I am first and foremost a collector. The writing is a part time profession and a hobby. The collecting of old toys is a passion. Like my three golden retrievers who constantly roam about the house with "things" in their mouths and who continually bring things to me when they don't even know why they do it, I collect things. I am not even sure why. And the things I collect are old toys.

One of the first considerations of any collector, advanced or novice, is "Where am I going to put all these toys!?" That's an interesting question which poses all kinds of pitfalls and possibilities. Most collectors don't purchase antique toy treasures just to hide them away; they usually purchase toys to display them. Collecting may bring the collector great adventure in the field, but ultimately it's the visual aspect of acquiring old toys that is so satisfying. We like to look at them. Museum curators learned long, long ago that heavy glass is a friend of the historian. Glass keeps danger from people, insects, dust, and even light out, and it keeps the items behind it safe and sound. Invest in glass. Buy cases with glass fronts that have solid closures. Buy all the glass front shelves and storage cases you can afford, even if it means sacrificing some toy purchases from time to time. Your collection will be the better for it. Glass is the toy collector's greatest friend. So is proper lighting. Lighting for collectibles is wonderful when it is built into fine display cabinets, but watch the temperature. Today's halogen lights burn very warm, and I have seen well meaning collectors put highly prized and valuable dolls on the top shelf of a halogen lit cabinet only to return and find cracked and damaged composition dolls that were literally baked in the hot oven of the display case. If a toy has even the remotest possibility of being damaged by heat, don't put it near the internal or recessed lighting of a display cabinet.

Directional light from above and just slightly in front of a showcase is a wonderful way to light old toys. Collectors who know me well know that I am a theatre teacher and director by profession, and believe me, I know lighting. The old textbook adage of "45 degrees up and out" has always worked well in the theatre, meaning the 45 degree front lighting angle is perfect for illumination of actors upon a stage (or toys inside a showcase). That 45 degree angle allows for full illumination from the front and above, but it's just the right angle to eliminate glare from the glass in front. It's a perfect geometric balance of light and design. Try it. Install some strip lighting out and in front of your best showcases. You will be amazed at the results. A collection of antique toys can literally come to life when lit properly!

In just the same way that light can be a collector's friend, it can also be an enemy. I have learned this lesson the hard way. Over the years, I have kept many of my best antique toy lithographed games and books on display on open shelves high on the walls. None of these are in direct line of light from the sun as a full length front porch shades our entire house and all the front exposure windows. Just the same, plenty of ultraviolet light filters into our house indirectly, and over a 10 to 15 year period, some of my finest antique toy games and lithographed books have slowly faded to less than attractive colors. One particularly horrifying lesson I learned concerned a rare Mickey Mouse Pop Gun Set that I purchased some 25 years ago and paid a dear price for. I purchased it for around $450 in the early 1980s and proudly displayed this impressive piece high on a shelf (not behind glass!) just around the corner from an indirectly sunlit window. I repeat, it was indirect sunlight. The game never (even in the summer) was exposed to direct sunlight...just bright indirect sun an hour or two a day. A couple of years ago, I took the game down to dust it, and over a decade and a half, the deep green background of this beautiful game manufactured by Marks Brothers of Boston, Massachusetts, in the 1930s had gradually faded to an ugly light pea green gradually and right before my eyes. And the damage was so steady and so gradual, I had not even noticed it. I sold the game to a buyer who was aware of the damage for around $300, but the target set would have been worth around $1,000 today. Aside from being an important $700 lesson, it was a real tragedy for the toy. And it was my own fault.

Sunlight is the greatest enemy of toys. I repeat and will capitalize it, SUNLIGHT IS THE GREATEST ENEMY OF TOYS! It is far more damaging than rust, because ultraviolet light damage creeps up on the toy and can never be reversed. Rust can be stopped, halted. There is no cure for ultraviolet light damage and its ugly fading effects upon old lithography of both tin and paper toys is relentless. Keep your toys behind glass which helps reflect away ultraviolet light and keep them away from even indirectly sunlit windows. May my $700 mistake save your own collection's value.

Now, back to the glass. Make sure showcases have a tight seal, and if insects like dust mites or moths are a problem in your particular climate, make sure you keep them away from your toys. Moths don't just like wool, they love old glue present in composition toys and paper lithographed books and boxes. They suck up glue-soaked pulp like it is turkey and gravy on Thanksgiving. After a lengthy summer vacation one year, I returned in horror to find that one single moth had devoured the complete soles of the felt shoes of a Doc the Dwarf (from Disney's Snow White) doll that I owned, had eaten up his wool beard until all that was left was a wool stubble and then for dessert had crunched away on the glue-soaked composition nose of the doll. Thankfully, the moth had expired from overeating and was dead at the dwarf's feet. He didn't damage any of the other dolls in the case. But if he hadn't died, he would have. They are stinky and unpleasant, but a single moth ball in the back of that showcase will prevent such dreaded moments. Be on guard.

Regarding storage of paper items, make sure you use archival worthy products. Acid-free papers and inert plastics that won't melt or interact with antique inks and paper pulps are available at fine scrapbooking

and stationary stores. Even comic book dealers know the merits of proper paper storage so seek these dealers out if there is one in your area. Anyone who knows about paper preservation can be helpful, and unless you are a museum curator or an archeologist, you need help. Make sure books are sealed off from insects, humidity, and extreme heat. Remember that such toy materials as rubber, paper, wool, and wood are all organic, and nothing organic lasts forever. It's a scientific fact. But proper preservation methods now can extend the life of antique toys when they are given care.

A key word to mention here is preservation, not restoration. Restoration is needed when a toy is purchased that needs serious repair, and preservation is the management technique administered so that eventual restoration is never needed. So remember: preservation, not restoration. Keep those words in mind and your collection will have a long life.

So, why not restoration? Aren't restored toys nicer to look at and more stable in the long haul once they are brought back up to speed? Yes, they are. But once restored, always restored. Watch any episode of the popular PBS series *Antiques Roadshow* and you will quickly learn what restoration does to the value of any antique. Toys are certainly no exception. Yes, restoration makes badly damaged toys nicer to look at, and yes, restoration will help preserve them. But it is a fact of life in the collecting world that collectors prefer not to purchase restorations. The problem is, it is often difficult to discern where restoration begins and ends. Is a toy a total repaint example, or just partial repaint? Does it have all new replacement parts or just a few? A toy that needs no conditional apologies is a toy that rests cleaner on the conscience of its owner. Buy a toy that is in 100% original excellent condition, and that's a toy you will never have to buy again. Buy mint condition when you can afford it, and you never have to buy again. If a toy goes into your collection as mint, it is

impossible to need an upgrade. You have saved yourself big dollars in the long run since you don't have to load and unload toy examples by trading and upgrading and retrading only to find yet a better example later. Buy mint and you buy once. So, avoid restorations, and buy mint toys whenever you can possibly afford them. Your collection (and your sanity) will be all the better for it!

Another commonly overlooked aspect of maintaining a successful collection throughout many decades is insurance. Nearly every collector in America lives within an area of some major disaster threat, be it hurricanes, earthquakes, fire, flood, or even tornadoes. Toy collections don't last under any of these circumstances, and theft is an even greater threat. Make sure your insurance riders on your home owner's policies are up to date to keep pace with the growth of your collecting habits. Most standard home owner's policies offer little or no replacement values for collectibles...those have to be protected and provided for with additional insurance riders and loads of documentation, but in the long run it is worth it. If you are willing to sink thousands of dollars annually into collecting antique toys, then surely it is worth several hundred dollars a year to protect yourself from significant financial loss should the unthinkable happen. And keep good records. Video record your entire collection, case by case and wall to wall. It may seem ridiculous as you are doing it, but realize that in the event of a natural disaster or a major theft, it will be important to be able to reconstruct what your collection looked like once upon a time. If you won't do it for yourself, do it for me. As an author who benefits from your purchase of this book, let me repay you by telling you to insure your collection today. There is no rational excuse for any other course of action. You must protect the investment you have made in your toys. Do it now! No excuses.

So, the checklist includes insure, display under glass, avoid ultraviolet light, preserve but don't restore, light properly and safely, and one more thing — control moisture. One of the worst places to keep a collection

is in a lower level room or basement that is subject to moisture. If you must keep the toys down there, control the humidity with continuous use of dehumidifiers. If you can't control the moisture problems in a basement or lower level, then move the toys. Rust works more quickly than ultraviolet light and its devastating effects upon tin lithographed toys is unavoidable. Even waxing tin toys won't help them if they are continually subject to humid air. Keep your books and your toys as dry as you possibly can. They will last longer, and so will your investment (and your sanity).

So, now that we have covered how to maintain your collection, let's discuss how to expand it. First and foremost, know your economics. If buying antique toys is putting your family seriously in debt, your collection won't last. Eventually you will find yourself "dumping" your collection into the marketplace to pay off debts and that's a quick way to lose what you have worked so hard to find. Slow and steady are the key words here. Buy mint condition toys when you can afford them, and if you can't buy mint, don't buy at all. Save for the next opportunity when you can buy mint. It takes willpower and discipline to come home empty handed from an antique toy show or auction, but if it means not putting yourself in the precarious situation of buying old toys you didn't have the money for it in the first place, then the pain of walking away is misery justified for a lesson well learned. Buy mint when you can afford it, and don't buy anything else when you can't afford mint. A small, pristine mint collection of old toys is worth far more than a whole house filled with worn out, damaged junk.

The Internet has opened up incredible possibilities for today's toy collector. Nearly everybody knows how to shop and sell on eBay now, but five years ago this was the exception and not the rule. Buying habits are volatile now, and as eBay's slogan continually reinforces, you can find "it" whenever you want it or need it, whatever "it" is. In the world of toy collecting, "it" is the next toy you just have to have for your collection.

Learn the ins and outs of Internet buying and make sure you have a recourse for a fouled-up purchase. It's buyer beware with most Internet purchases, but eBay's user feedback system allows for a spirit of honesty and cooperation to exist between buyer and seller on good days. But be forewarned: It can be very difficult to take action against a deal that has gone sour. If you live in New York City and your seller is in San Francisco, it's going to be tough to actually litigate if a real problem exists. Normally, bidders and buyers and sellers work through problems in a virtual spirit of cooperation trying to resolve problems for the common good. At least, that's the way eBay and everyone else hopes it will work.

Be patient as you bid, learn to use bidding strategies that are open and honest, not cutthroat. "Snipers" often lie in wait out there in cyberland just waiting to outbid you in the last seconds, so understand the eBay and other Internet site rules of the game, and then learn to play the game successfully. In the past eight years, a substantial portion of my own collecting has been through eBay and Internet purchases, and less has been from attending antique toy shows…and I miss that. Regardless of how much you love your computer, it will never replace the human link and satisfaction of building trust with live dealers at real antique shows. Nothing will ever replace that. So don't overlook the people out there who can put you in touch with great toys. They still exist. How do you find them? Read on.

The most commonly overlooked successful means of finding great antique toys is word of mouth. It seems so simple it looks ridiculous on the surface, but it works. Talk about what you collect to everyone you meet. You never know what people have hiding in their closets… really. Just last month, I was bemoaning the fact that there was one toy that had eluded me all these years, a Beanie character doll made by Mattel in the early 1960s and a toy I wanted badly on Christmas morning

in 1960. Usually Santa brought everything I wanted, I was a particularly good young lad and I communicated to Santa my wishes, down to even crayons and batteries when I needed them. But somehow in 1960, either I or Santa, or both of us slipped up. There was no Beanie. (In later years, I came to believe that my Dad may have seen Beanie as a doll, and he didn't want me to have a doll. But I will never know for sure.) Anyway, I was whining to an antique dealer friend that I am now 52, have just recovered from quintuple heart bypass surgery nine months ago, and I still don't have my Beanie. Now this sounds ridiculous (and is!) except for the fact that I was being honest and had always avoided buying one because those darn little dolls are always missing their cute propellers on top. I told my good friend my woes, and three days later, she found one at a half-off post-holiday sale in absolute mint condition at the local D. A. V. thrift store. I mean, the little guy is just-off-the-store-shelf-like-in-1960-mint! She bought him so "right" that she just gave him to me! (Probably to end my whining!)

So, as I sit here in my study typing away on my Dell, Beanie is now smiling his quirky grin and staring at me. But, I've got him. And for some really odd reason, I feel better because he is here. Maybe it's my mortality that I'm facing because of the heart surgery, or maybe it's my blood pressure medicine kicking in, but I would swear that both he knows and I know we were eventually supposed to end up together. But I had to wait nearly 46 years! I use this illustration to drive home the point that you need to talk to everyone whom you meet (and trust) that toy collecting is an important part of your life. As you share, and they share, you will be amazed at what unusual antique toys might just "emerge" from the shadows of old basements, attics, garages, and closets. Somebody you know may have just what you are looking for. Don't be shy. Talk about your toys.

How else can you expand your toy horizons? Don't overlook the power of the country auction on a bad weather day. If the crowd is down, so may be the prices. Elmer and Viola Reynolds of Indiana who contributed many toys from their wonderful collections to this book once headed to a remote country auction on a snowy day and left a bid on the Mickey Mouse Marks Brothers Piano mint in a mint box. I believe their left bid was around $200, and it won the toy. Even on a bad day, the piano should have brought $1,000 two decades ago. Now it is worth thousands. And they have it all because they went to that auction when the weather was lousy.

Yard sales produce wonderful toys, too, if (and that's a big if) you are lucky enough to be the first guy there. It's worth a shot, but it's a long shot. And yard sale scouring eats up tanks of gas with very few treasures ever found. Certainly huge outdoor antique extravaganzas like the annual ones held in Springfield, Ohio, each year still draw thousands of dealers and tens of thousands of buyers. Brimfield Summer Shows in Brimfield, Massachusetts, are still a happy hunting ground for wonderful antique toys, but under priced bargains are getting harder and harder to find there. There's just so much competition now. The year round St. Charles Toy Shows billed as the Antique Toy and Doll World Shows are still worth a weekend in northern Illinois, but the rare stuff seems to have already been discovered decades ago. The Internet seems to have changed everything…or has it?

What may have really changed is what we are looking for. When I was in my twenties, I looked for that toy that I thought was under priced and rare. In my thirties, I looked for that which was just rare. In my forties, I looked for whatever I thought would be a toy I might not ever see again, and now that I am in my fifties, I am always looking to find…my shoes. It is all a matter of timing and perspectives.

But, we stay on the hunt for those great old toys, don't we? Why? Maybe it is genetic. Some switch in our brain has clicked on and we don't know how to switch it off. Like my golden retrievers, we run after our toys because we find joy in just bringing them back, for no apparent reason. And tomorrow, we will do the same all over again….just because it is fun, and feels good.

You can learn a lot from watching your dogs. Beanie is still smiling at me, and my goldens are each chomping on a squishy toy…all three of them. We are all four of us true collectors, and we still don't know why. But it's still fun. Life is good.

Enjoy your days of collecting in the time you have left!

— David Longest, February 2007

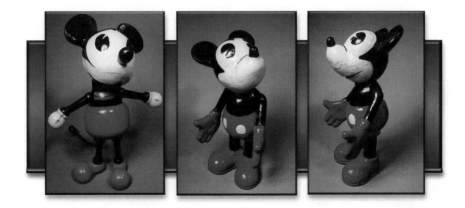

ABOUT THE AUTHOR

DAVID LONGEST IS THE AUTHOR OF SIX PREVIOUS BOOKS on collecting antique toys published by Collector Books: *Character Toys and Collectibles* (1984), *Character Toys and Collectibles, Series Two* (1986), T*oys — Antique and Collectible* (1988), *The Collector's Encyclopedia of Disneyana* (with Michael Stern, 1991), *Antique Toys — 1870 to 1960* (1993), and *Cartoon Toys and Collectibles* (1997). In 2007, two new books by Longest will be released: *Collecting Disneyana* and *The Toy Yearbook*. David is proud to have been a Collector Books author for over a quarter of a century!

Longest has written nationally for several magazines including *Collector's Showcase, Antique Trader, The Tristate Trader,* and *Antique Toy World.* He served as a monthly feature writer and contributing editor for *Toy Shop* magazine in the 1990s.

David's full time job is serving as a teacher and director of theatre at New Albany High School in Indiana where he is an award-winning teacher with an award-winning theatre program. His program was awarded the National Outstanding High School Theatre Award by the Educational Theatre Association in 2004. Longest was selected as the New Albany Floyd County Teacher of the Year and as Indiana Teacher of the Year semi-finalist the same year. David is additionally the recipient of two Lilly Endowment Teacher Creativity Awards and the WHAS-TV Excel Award for Outstanding Teaching. Longest is also one of few high school teachers in the nation to win the prestigious National American History Medal awarded by the D.A.R. in Washington, D.C., which he won for co-authoring an original musical on Lewis and Clark and his adaptation of Little Women, published by Dramatic Publishing of Chicago, Illinois. Longest has been a guest lecturer on Broadway in New York for Broadway Classroom, and he and his students were featured in a three-page article in *The New York Times* in May of 2005. Additionally, David Longest and his students are soon to be featured in a 2008 motion picture documentary release by Lions Gate Pictures of Hollywood (directed by Barry Blaustein) devoted to exemplary high school musical theatre programs. Most recently, Longest was selected by Music Theatre International and Walt Disney Theatricals as one of very few pilot premiere directors in the nation to produce an early production of Disney's High School Musical which will be featured at the International Thespian Festival this year in Lincoln, Nebraska. David's former students have appeared in nearly two dozen Broadway, London West End, and American National Theatre tours. David has been a teacher for 30 years.